A SHAKESPEARE MERRIMENT

GARLAND REFERENCE LIBRARY
OF THE HUMANITIES
(VOL. 836)

"My love, who said 'Brevity is the soul of wit'?"   "You did, of course, dear."

Drawing by Bernard Schoenbaum; © 1985 The New Yorker Magazine, Inc..

A SHAKESPEARE MERRIMENT
An Anthology of Shakespearean Humor

Edited by
Marilyn Schoenbaum

GARLAND PUBLISHING, INC. • NEW YORK & LONDON
1988

Library of Congress Cataloging-in-Publication Data

A Shakespeare merriment: an anthology of Shakespearean humor /
[compiled and edited by] Marilyn Schoenbaum.
    p. cm — (Garland reference library of the humanities; vol. 836)
Includes index.
ISBN 0–8240–5738–4 (alk. paper)
    1. Shakespeare, William, 1564–1616—Literary collections.
2. Shakespeare, William, 1564–1616—Appreciation.   3. English wit
and humor.   4. American wit and humor.   6. English literature.
6. American literature.   I. Schoenbaum, Marilyn.   II. Series.
PR2925.S53   1988
822.3'3—dc19   88–11132
                                                                        CIP

Printed on acid-free, 250-year-life paper
Manufactured in the United States of America

For
S.

CONTENTS

FOREWORD

All in the family. My wife Marilyn and I have been enjoying
Shakespearean encounters since the Cretaceous era—or so it
seems—when we met in a special high school English class
in a then sedate lower-middle-class neighborhood in the
South Bronx, the district that has since gained notoriety as
Fort Apache. We began dating then. One of the first
performances we took in together was of the Margaret
Webster production of *Othello* (a play neither of us had yet
read), with Paul Robeson in the title role, and the young
José Ferrer, an as yet unknown quantity, playing a
diabolically ingratiating Iago. Not long after, we eloped.
We still have the tattered program. When, not long ago, we
met Ferrer socially in the Great Hall of the Folger
Shakespeare Library in Washington, my wife brought along
the program for him to autograph; maybe it pays to keep old
programs.

Perhaps it was inevitable that Marilyn would in time
produce her own Shakespearean opus: a collection of
variegated pieces testifying to the hold that the supreme
western cultural hero has maintained over writers, amateur
and professional, who followed in his wake. Ms. S.'s
selections range from the off-the-cuff anecdote set down by

John Manningham (a law student who lived contemporaneously with Shakespeare) to a host of what the editor refers to as Shakespearean afterimages. Some are the offspring of writers who are themselves great—the excerpts from Fielding and Dickens, for example—but the inventory does not exclude the occasionally scurrilous: witness "The Skinhead Hamlet." Considerations of space have sometimes made it necessary for the editor to omit items that she would otherwise have very much liked to include—for example, Henry James's substantial novella, *The Birthplace*—or to give only a portion of an item she would have wished to provide in its entirety, e.g., Tom Stoppard's *Rosencrantz and Guildenstern Are Dead.* For there has been God's plenty from which to choose: the gamut of Shakespearean afterimages is, unsurprisingly, astonishing—if something unsurprising can be said to be astonishing, and Marilyn has sought to assemble a representative selection.

A Shakespeare Merriment she calls her book, fully aware that not all the items are by any means notable for their hilarity, although some are. But all testify to the pleasures of such encounters. Coming upon James Thurber's "The Macbeth Murder Mystery" is like having a reunion with an old friend. The compiler very much enjoyed bringing her collection together and devoutly hopes that her Merriment may indeed be a source of merriment.

S. Schoenbaum
Center for Renaissance and Baroque Studies
University of Maryland

PREFACE

Shakespeare has always been a presence in my life, as he has been for others. As a high school student, I sleepwalked and rubbed my hands as Lady Macbeth. When, later on, I did some professional acting, I always set playing Shakespeare as my goal. The Shakespearean virus infected my husband too: he became a professional Shakespearean. Eventually, about a decade ago, we found ourselves in the promised land in our own lifetimes: we live now on Capitol Hill, within walking distance of the Folger Shakespeare Library and the Library of Congress. The scene being thus set, it was inevitable that one day I should myself produce a book on Shakespeare. I hope that reading this collection gives as much pleasure as I had in producing it.

There were many people who were most helpful and supportive with their suggestions and encouragement during the preparation of *A Shakespeare Merriment*. I would like to express special thanks to Joan and Peter Andrews, John Andrews, Ann Jennalie Cook, Hardy Cook, Caroline Cooper, Marcus Cunliffe, John Fuegi, Donna Hamilton, Sidney Homan, Seymour and Anita Isenberg, Sean and Ceci Magee, Louis Marder, Irvin Matus, Diane McLennan, Adriana and Oliver Orr, Roberta Sabban, John Walley,

Brian Waltham, Jane Weinberger, and Ian Willison. Also to the librarians at the British Library and the Library of Congress, and to Alfred B. Maury at my local public library, who assisted me when I needed help. The people at the Folger Shakespeare Library were particularly helpful. I must mention Janel Feierabend, Anita Fox, Phillip Knachel, Jean Miller, Betsy Walsh, and, of course, the Director, Werner Gundersheimer. At Garland Publishing Gary Kuris and Phyllis Korper lightened my burden with their expertise and solicitude. Diane Clark furnished typing assistance beyond the call of duty. And very special thanks are in order to my brother-in-law, Bernard Schoenbaum, the *New Yorker* cartoonist, for letting me grace the pages of this book with his Shakespearean cartoon.

I would like to express my deepest appreciation to my husband S. for his persistence in nudging me to get this show finished and on the road. Whatever deficiencies this collection may have are, of course, my responsibility alone.

M.S.
Washington, D.C.
January 1988

INTRODUCTION

In *Henry IV, Part 2*, Falstaff claims to his page, "I am not only witty in myself, but the cause that wit is in other men" (Act I, sc. ii). If that is true of Falstaff, so is it true of Falstaff's creator, as has been abundantly demonstrated for almost four centuries. For Shakespeare has been the source of inspiration for many writers. He has been an influence for the creations of others in such diverse literary endeavors as verse, long and short stories, travesties, spoonerisms, puns, anecdotes, conundrums, novels, limericks, parodies, travel writings, and even cartoons, jokes, and plays. His plays have been translated into innumerable ballets, operas, films, and television screenings. He has inspired practically every writer of note. Some are themselves great artists; others, lesser fry. This book presents some of their relevant writings. As a pre-eminent cultural hero, Shakespeare became the source (rarely the butt) of a multitude of jokes and funny stories; but that is the subject of another book. Of more profound consequence is Shakespeare as the continuing source of wit—to be sure, considered broadly—in the writers who followed him.

This collection brings together pieces testifying to Shakespeare's influence on subsequent writers; afterimages of Shakespeare, as I term them. The anthology is by no means definitive and is meant to entertain. It covers a period of almost four centuries and is arranged in roughly chronological order, starting with John Manningham's famous anecdote, often retold, of the dramatist's amorous triumph with a citizen's wife over the great actor Richard Burbage, and is catholic enough to include Richard Curtis's outrageous modern parody, "The Skinhead Hamlet."

A friend of Dr. Johnson who eked out a precarious livelihood by turning out reviews, compilations, abridgements, translations, etc., Oliver Goldsmith yet achieved enduring fame as a poet (*The Deserted Village*), dramatist (*She Stoops to Conquer*), and novelist (*The Vicar of Wakefield*). Goldsmith's voluminous writings—the modern collected edition comes to five substantial volumes—did not entirely escape the presence of Shakespearean after-images. In his *A Reverie at the Boar's-head-tavern in Eastcheap*, Goldsmith owns that "The character of old Falstaff, even with all his faults, gives me more consolation than the most studied efforts of wisdom." As the reverie proceeds, his host transmutes into Mistress Quickly as the author sits dozing in the tavern which, he says, is still kept at Eastcheap. Actually the tavern was destroyed in the Great Fire of 1666, but at once rebuilt, and remained open until it was finally demolished in 1831. The vision of Mistress Quickly tells of how the tavern became a monastery after she was laid in the dust, and, in time, was once again a tavern until the last mistress of note, Jane Rouse, was condemned in the Old Bailey for witchcraft. Other revelations follow (the tavern was for a time a brothel) until the reverie has run its course, providing not a romance but a description of the spirit of the times. That had been Goldsmith's purpose all along.

In his day Washington Irving was known as the "American Goldsmith," and was the first American writer to gain an international reputation. He lived in Europe for seventeen years, and during that time wrote *The Sketch Book of Geoffrey Crayon, Gent.* (1819–20). It contains the famous "Rip Van Winkle" and "The Legend of Sleepy Hollow" tales. How fortunate it is that Irving also included in the *Sketch Book* an account of his visit to Stratford-upon-Avon! Irving captivates the reader with his description of this visit—from the "garrulous old lady" who shows him round Shakespeare's birthplace—to his ramble through the park at Carlecote (which Irving spells "Charlecot"), where Shakespeare, tradition holds, poached Sir Thomas Lucy's deer and fled to London—and the stage—to avoid prosecution. We meet native Stratfordians on their own turf and see Shakespeare country through Irving's eyes, which, I might add, have a decided twinkle in them.

This anthology also includes chapters from *Tom Jones* and *Great Expectations*. Both Henry Fielding and Charles Dickens responded to the lure of the theater, and had characters in their novels attend a performance of *Hamlet*. Fielding was a friend of David Garrick, the leading Shakespearean actor of the time. In *Tom Jones* Tom takes his simple-minded companion Partridge, Mrs. Miller, and her youngest daughter to a performance of *Hamlet*, "acted by the best player who ever was on the stage." Partridge, who until now has only seen country acting, is critical of the performance, preferring the king to Hamlet. To amuse and enlighten his own actor-friend, Fielding has written this chapter with tongue in cheek. Dickens, as a young man, thought of becoming an actor and did produce amateur theatricals. In *Great Expectations* Pip and his friend Herbert go to see Mr. Wopsle, who is a friend of the family that brought up Pip, and thinks he is destined to be an actor and to perform *Hamlet*. Dickens, with his special feeling and enthusiasm for the theater, knows whereof he speaks. In his mid-thirties, in 1848, the already famous author of *Oliver Twist* and *A Christmas Carol* acted Justice Shallow in a series of benefit performances of *The Merry Wives of Windsor* in Manchester, Liverpool, and Birmingham, and in Edinburgh and Glasgow.

Shakespearean after-images surface in such diversely gifted masters as Mark Twain and George Bernard Shaw. All readers will recall the king and the duke as, floating down the Mississippi, they get up *Romeo and Juliet* by heart and, with unwitting hilarity, rehearse Hamlet's "sublime" soliloquy for their "Shakespeare Revival! ! !" in a one-horse "Arkansaw" town in *The Adventures of Huckleberry Finn*. This revival is destined never to take place. Wandering minstrels and charlatans—as Twain was well aware—had performed similar feats in other one-horse towns; a distinctive manifestation, scrupulously evoked, of the Shakespearean heritage in nineteenth-century outback America.

Not Stratford folk but a Shakespearean presence occupied George Bernard Shaw when, almost a century later, Shaw wrote *The Dark Lady of the Sonnets*, performed at the Haymarket Theatre in London's West End in November 1910 for the purpose of helping to raise money for a National Theatre "as a memorial to Shakespeare"—so Shaw himself explains in his Preface. In addition to the Dark Lady, here conceived as Mistress Mary Fitton, this modest playlet offers Queen Elizabeth and Shakespeare himself as characters. The great Harley Granville-Barker appropriately played Shakespeare. But the *pièce de résistance* of the *pièce d'occasion* is Shaw's prefatory evocation of the unforgettable Thomas Tyler.

Oscar Wilde, who when embarking on his triumphant American tour had informed a customs inspector that he had nothing to declare but his genius, declared it in a minor key with his "Portrait of Mr W. H." Reproduced here is the shorter first version—today no longer convenient of access—published by Wilde in *Blackwood's Edinburgh Magazine* in 1889. The identity of this dedicatee of the Sonnets continues to engage scholarly attention, the most recent candidate (1986) being William Hathaway, Anne's brother. Wilde's more imaginative choice is Willie Hughes, a presumed boy actor in Shakespeare's troupe, of whom a full-length painting hangs in a London house. (The name is inspired by a play upon *hews* in Sonnet 20.) He wears a black velvet doublet and has white lily hands, this youth of girlish beauty. The next year Wilde would publish *The Picture of Dorian Gray*. In 1895 he was sentenced to two years' hard labor in Reading Gaol for homosexual offenses.

Shakespeare was for James Joyce "the playwright who wrote the Folio of the world." In the wonderfully complex interfacings (to use a term made current by today's word-processor technology) of *Ulysses*, the life, poems, and plays—most notably *Hamlet*, but most of the others too—loom large in Stephen Dedalus's consciousness: his unconscious too. Joyce devotes a whole section of *Ulysses*, the "Scylla and Charybdis" episode, to a discussion of Shakespeare's life and art. Stephen does not fail to mention the Manningham anecdote or Oscar Wilde's candidate for Mr. W. H., Willie Hughes. In the librarian's office of the National Library on Kildare Street of "dear dirty Dublin," Stephen gives his views on Shakespeare. The contributions of Sidney Lee, Georg Brandes, and Frank Harris leave their mark on the discourse, as does even the recent discovery by Charles W. Wallace of the dramatist as a matchmaker in London's Silver Street. For this collection I have included a passage from *Ulysses* especially rich in Shakespearean allusion as Stephen Dedalus holds forth on the fateful afternoon of June 16, 1904, the day now celebrated, wherever Joyce is revered, as Bloomsday.

Most celebrated, I suppose, for his tales of the Raj and *Barrack-Room Ballads*, Rudyard Kipling, who coined the phrase "the white man's burden," led a remarkably varied literary life, so perhaps it should come as no surprise that, shortly before his death, he was imagining Shakespeare and Ben Jonson sitting on heavy chairs beneath eaves of a summer house by the orchard, sipping wine, chatting about the playwriting scene, and fiddling with phrases in the proofs of the new King James version of the Bible in front of them—"The Proofs of Holy Writ" of Kipling's title. Shakespeare has given rise to some unpredictable after-images; for Kipling was inspired by another Will besides *Wee Willie Winkie*. The Stratford Will was for Kipling a light that never failed.

To demonstrate the range of Shakespearean after-images I have included a cornucopia of miscellaneous items: James Thurber's justly celebrated "The Macbeth Murder Mystery," which invites readers to look at a classic in a new way; Maurice Baring's "Lady Macbeth's Trouble," one of the delicious series of imaginary letters from which I only with difficulty limited my selection to a single exemplar; and Banesh Hoffman's "Shakespeare the Physicist," which invokes Sherlock Holmes's powers of deduction to demonstrate that Shakespeare anticipated the wireless, relativity, and the atomic bomb. In *The Education of H*Y*M*A*N K*A*P*L*A*N*, Leo Rosten gently caricatures American immigrant life when he has Mr. Kaplan encounter Julius Scissor in night school.

A more sophisticated, but in its own way no less humorous, world is evoked by Wolcott Gibbs, whose career as a writer is associated, throughout his lifetime, with *The New Yorker*, first as a staff member (from 1927), and then for eighteen years as the magazine's stylish drama critic, celebrated for his acerbic wit—but not as an enthusiast of Broadway's Shakespeare revivals (at a time when Broadway still had Shakespeare revivals). I include a piece from Gibbs's *Bed of Neuroses* entitled "Ring Out, Wild Bells," in which he recalls his debut as a child, playing Puck in *A Midsummer Night's Dream* on the open-air stage at the Riverdale Country School.

Also furnished is a substantial extract from Tom Stoppard's *Rosencrantz and Guildenstern Are Dead*. First performed August 24, 1966, at Cranston Street Hall, Edinburgh, by the Oxford Theatre Company's part of the "fringe" at the Edinburgh Festival, the play amply demonstrates the metaphysical wit for which the dramatist has become celebrated, as he places Shakespeare's "attendant Lords," only peripheral in *Hamlet*, at the center of the great and tragic events that preoccupied Shakespeare. Human solitude and impotence hauntingly work their spell. Stoppard was not yet thirty when *Rosencrantz and Guildenstern Are Dead* made its debut. He was now famous, and would remain so. Shakespeare's life naturally finds a place in Manson Myers's *From Beowulf to Virginia Woolf* and Richard Armour's *Twisted Tales from Shakespeare*, and Caryl Brahms and S.J. Simon sport with the naming of the Globe Theatre in *No Bed for Bacon*. In "The Kugelmass Episode" in Woody Allen's *Side Effects*, Persky for a double sawbuck hilariously uses a time machine to bring Madame Bovary to the Plaza Hotel in New York; in what is not more than a fictional anecdote the inexhaustibly prolific Isaac Asimov, in *Earth Is Room Enough: Science Fiction Tales of Our Own Planet*, similarly transports the Immortal Bard, not to the Plaza, however, but to an ordinary classroom. In "But Soft . . . Real Soft," in *Without Feathers*, Allen had his own fleeting encounter with, as he puts it, "The Immortal Bard of Stratford on Avon" or, more precisely, with anti-Stratfordianism. I was at a conference in Trivandrum, in southernmost India, when a don there from the University of Bombay heard about my project and drew my attention to Don Marquis's *archy and mehitabel*, in which archy, the poetical cockroach, and mehitabel, the Bohemian cat, engagingly hold forth. The works of archy and mehitabel include "pete the parrot and shakespeare." Bernard Shaw or James Joyce these artists may not be, but all and sundry testify to the ubiquitousness in our literary culture of Shakespearean afterimages.

A Shakespeare Merriment

WILLIAM THE CONQUEROR ANECDOTE

John Manningham

Upon a time when Burbage played Richard the Third there was a citizen grew so far in liking with him, that before she went from the play she appointed him to come that night unto her by the name of Richard the Third. Shakespeare, overhearing their conclusion, went before, was entertained and at his game ere Burbage came. Then message being brought that Richard the Third was at the door, Shakespeare caused return to be made that William the Conqueror was before Richard the Third.

Manningham informatively adds, "Shakespeare's name William."

The Humble Situation of Shakespeare. Courtesy of the Folger Shakespeare Library, Washington, D. C.

SHAKESPEARE AS HORSEHOLDER

Samuel Johnson

In the time of Elizabeth, coaches being yet uncommon, and hired coaches not at all in use, those who were too proud, too tender, or too idle to walk, went on horseback to any distant business or diversion. Many came on horseback to the play, and when Shakespeare fled to London from the terror of a criminal prosecution, his first expedient was to wait at the door of the playhouse, and hold the horses of those that had no servants, that they might be ready again after the performance. In this office he became so conspicuous for his care and readiness, that in a short time every man as he alighted called for Will Shakespeare, and scarcely any other waiter was trusted with a horse while Will Shakespeare could be had. This was the first dawn of better fortune. Shakespeare finding more horses put into his hand than he could hold, hired boys to wait under his inspection, who, when Will Shakespeare was summoned, were immediately to present themselves, "I am Shakespeare's boy, Sir." In time Shakespeare found higher employment, but as long as the practice of riding to the playhouse continued, the waiters that hold the horses retained the appellation of Shakespeare's Boys.

From *TOM JONES*

Henry Fielding

In the first row, then, of the first gallery did Mr. Jones, Mrs. Miller, her youngest daughter, and Partridge take their places. Partridge immediately declared it was the finest place he had ever been in. When the first music was played, he said, "It was a wonder how so many fiddlers could play at one time, without putting one another out." While the fellow was lighting the upper candles, he cried out to Mrs. Miller, "Look, look, madam, the very picture of the man in the end of the common-prayer book before the gunpowder-treason service." Nor could he help observing, with a sigh, when all the candles were lighted, "That here were candles enough burnt in one night, to keep an honest poor family for a whole twelve-month."

As soon as the play, which was Hamlet, Prince of Denmark, began, Partridge was all attention, nor did he break silence till the entrance of the ghost; upon which he asked Jones, "What man that was in the strange dress; something," said he, "like what I have seen in a picture. Sure it is not armour, is it"—Jones answered, "That is the ghost."—To which Partridge replied with a smile, "Persuade me to that, sir, if you can. Though I can't say I ever actually saw a ghost in my life, yet I am certain I should know one, if I saw him, better than that comes to. No, no, sir, ghosts don't appear in such dresses as that, neither." In this mistake, which caused much laughter in the neighbourhood of Partridge, he was suffered to continue, till the scene between the ghost and Hamlet, when Partridge gave that credit to Mr. Garrick which he had denied to Jones, and fell into so violent a trembling, that his knees knocked against each other. Jones asked him what was the matter, and whether he was afraid of the warrior upon the stage? "O la! sir," said he, "I perceive now it is what you told me. I am not afraid of anything; for I know it is but a play. And if it was really a ghost, it could do no one harm at such a distance, and in so much company; and yet if I was frightened, I am not the only person."—"Why, who," cries Jones, "dost thou take to be such a coward here besides thyself?"—"Nay, you may call me coward if you will; but if that little man there upon the stage is not frightened, I never saw any man frightened in my life. Ay, ay: go along with you: ay, to be sure! Who's fool then? Will you? Lud have mercy upon such foolhardiness!—Whatever happens, it is good enough for you.——Follow you? I'd follow the devil as soon. Nay, perhaps it is the devil——for they say he can put on what likeness he pleases.—Oh! here he is again.——No farther! No, you have gone far enough already; farther than I'd have gone for all the king's dominions." Jones offered to speak, but Partridge cried, "Hush, hush! dear sir, don't you hear him?" And during the whole speech of the ghost, he sat with his eyes fixed partly on the ghost and partly on Hamlet, and with his mouth open; the same passions which succeeded each other in Hamlet succeeding likewise in him.

When the scene was over Jones said, "Why, Partridge, you exceed my expectations. You enjoy the play more than I conceived possible."—"Nay, sir," answered Partridge, "if you are not afraid of the devil, I can't help it; but, to be sure, it is natural to be surprised at such things, though I know there is nothing in them: not that it was the ghost that surprised me, neither; for I should have known that to have been only a man in a strange dress; but when I saw the little man so frightened himself, it was that which took hold of

me."—"And dost thou imagine, then, Partridge," cries
Jones, "that he was really frightened?"—"Nay, sir," said
Partridge, "did not you yourself observe afterwards, when
he found it was his own father's spirit, and how he was
murdered in the garden, how his fear forsook him by
degrees, and he was struck dumb with sorrow, as it were,
just as I should have been, had it been my own case?—But
hush! O la! what noise is that? There he is again.—Well, to
be certain, though I know there is nothing at all in it, I am
glad I am not down yonder, where those men are." Then
turning his eyes again upon Hamlet, "Ay, you may draw
your sword; what signifies a sword against the power of the
devil?"

During the second act, Partridge made very few remarks.
He greatly admired the fineness of the dresses; nor could he
help observing upon the king's countenance. "Well," said
he, "how people may be deceived by faces! *Nulla fides
fronti* is, I find, a true saying. Who would think, by looking
in the king's face, that he had ever committed a murder?" He
then inquired after the ghost; but Jones, who intended he
should be surprised, gave him no other satisfaction than
"that he might possibly see him again soon, and in a flash of
fire."

Partridge sat in a fearful expectation of this; and now,
when the ghost made his next appearance, Partridge cried
out, "There, sir, now; what say you now? is he frightened
now or no? As much frightened as you think me, and, to be
sure, nobody can help some fears. I would not be in so bad
a condition as what's his name, squire Hamlet, is there, for
all the world. Bless me! what's become of the spirit? As I
am a living soul, I thought I saw him sink into the earth."—
"Indeed, you saw right," answered Jones.—"Well, well,"
cries Partridge, "I know it is only a play; and besides, if
there was anything in all this, Madam Miller would not laugh
so; for, as to you, sir, you would not be afraid, I believe, if
the devil was here in person.—There, there—Ay, no
wonder you are in such a passion; shake the vile wicked
wretch to pieces. If she was my own mother, I would serve
her so. To be sure, all duty to a mother is forfeited by such

wicked doings.—Ay, go about your business, I hate the sight of you."

Our critic was now pretty silent till the play which Hamlet introduces before the king. This he did not at first understand, till Jones explained it to him; but he no sooner entered into the spirit of it than he began to bless himself that he had never committed murder. Then turning to Mrs. Miller, he asked her, "If she did not imagine the king looked as if he was touched; though he is," said he, "a good actor, and doth all he can to hide it. Well, I would not have so much to answer for as that wicked man there hath, to sit upon a much higher chair than he sits upon. No wonder he run away; for your sake I'll never trust an innocent face again."

The grave-digging scene next engaged the attention of Partridge, who expressed much surprise at the number of skulls thrown upon the stage. To which Jones answered, "That it was one of the most famous burial-places about town."—"No wonder, then," cries Partridge, "that the place is haunted. But I never saw in my life a worse grave-digger. I had a sexton, when I was clerk, that should have dug three graves while he is digging one. The fellow handles a spade as if it was the first time he had ever had one in his hand. Ay, ay, you may sing. You had rather sing than work, I believe."—Upon Hamlet's taking up the skull, he cried out, "Well! it is strange to see how fearless some men are: I never could bring myself to touch anything belonging to a dead man, on any account.—He seemed frightened enough too at the ghost, I thought. *Nemo omnibus horis sapit.*"

Little more worth remembering occurred during the play, at the end of which Jones asked him, "Which of the players he had liked best?" To this he answered, with some appearance of indignation at the question, "The king, without doubt."—"Indeed, Mr. Partridge," says Mrs. Miller. "You are not of the same opinion with the town; for they are all agreed that Hamlet is acted by the best player who ever was on the stage."—"He the best player!" cries Partridge, with a contemptuous sneer; "why, I could act as well as he myself. I am sure, if I had seen a ghost, I should have looked in the very same manner, and done just as he did. And then, to be sure, in that scene, as you called, between him and his mother, where you told me he acted so fine, why, Lord help me, any man, that is, any good man, that had such a mother, would have done exactly the same. I know you are only joking with me; but indeed, madam, though I was never at a play in London, yet I have seen acting before in the country: and the king for my money; he speaks all his words distinctly, half as loud again as the other.—Anybody may see he is an actor."

While Mrs. Miller was thus engaged in conversation with Partridge, a lady came up to Mr. Jones, whom he immediately knew to be Mrs. Fitzpatrick. She said, she had seen him from the other part of the gallery, and had taken that opportunity of speaking to him, as she had something to say which might be of great service to himself. She then acquainted him with her lodgings, and made him an appointment the next day in the morning; which, upon recollection, she presently changed to the afternoon; at which time Jones promised to attend her.

Thus ended the adventure at the playhouse; where Partridge had afforded great mirth, not only to Jones and Mrs. Miller, but to all who sat within hearing, who were more attentive to what he said than to anything that passed on the stage.

He durst not go to bed all that night, for fear of the ghost; and for many nights after sweated two or three hours before he went to sleep, with the same apprehensions, and waked several times in great horrors, crying out, "Lord have mercy upon us! there it is."

A REVERIE AT THE BOAR'S-HEAD-TAVERN IN EASTCHEAP

Oliver Goldsmith

The improvements we make in mental acquirements, only render us each day more sensible of the defects of our constitution: with this in view, therefore, let us often recur to the amusements of youth; endeavour to forget age and wisdom, and, as far as innocence goes, be as much a boy as the best of them.

Let idle declaimers mourn over the degeneracy of the age; but, in my opinion, every age is the same. This I am sure of, that man, in every season, is a poor fretful being, with no other means to escape the calamities of the times but by endeavouring to forget them; for, if he attempts to resist, he is certainly undone. If I feel poverty and pain, I am not so hardy as to quarrel with the executioner, even while under correction: I find myself no way disposed to make fine speeches, while I am making wry faces. In a word, let me drink when the fit is on, to make me insensible; and drink when it is over, for joy that I feel pain no longer.

The character of old Falstaff, even with all his faults, gives me more consolation than the most studied efforts of wisdom: I here behold an agreeable old fellow, forgetting age, and shewing me the way to be young at sixty-five. Sure I am well able to be as merry, though not so comical as he.—Is it not in my power to have, though not so much wit, at least as much vivacity? Age, care, wisdom, reflection, begone—I give you to the winds. Let's have t'other bottle: here's to the memory of Shakespear, Falstaff, and all the merry men of East-cheap.

Such were the reflections that naturally arose while I sat at the Boar's-head tavern, still kept at East-cheap. Here, by a pleasant fire, in the very room where old Sir John Falstaff cracked his jokes, in the very chair which was sometimes honoured by prince Henry and sometimes polluted by his immoral merry companion, I sat, and ruminated on the follies of youth; wished to be young again; but was resolved to make the best of life while it lasted, and now and then compared past and present times together. I considered myself as the only living representative of the old Knight, and transported my imagination back to the times when the Prince and he gave life to the revel, and made even debauchery not disgusting. The room also conspired to throw my reflections back into antiquity: the oak-floor, the Gothic windows, and the ponderous chimney-piece, had long withstood the tooth of time: the watchman had gone twelve: my companions had all stolen off, and none now remained with me but the landlord. From him I could have wished to know the history of a tavern that had such a long succession of customers: I could not help thinking that an account of this kind would be a pleasing contrast of the manners of different ages; but my landlord could give me no information. He continued to doze and sot, and tell a tedious story, as most other landlords usually do; and, though he said nothing, yet was never silent: one good joke followed another good joke; and the best joke of all was generally begun towards the end of a bottle. I found at last, however, his wine and his conversation operate by degrees: he insensibly began to alter his appearance. His cravat seemed quilled into a ruff, and his breeches swelled out into a fardingale. I now fancied him changing sexes; and, as my eyes began to close in slumber, I imagined my fat landlord actually converted into as fat a landlady. However, sleep made but few changes in my situation: the tavern, the apartment, and the table continued as before; nothing suffered mutation but my host, who was fairly altered into a gentlewoman, whom I knew to be Dame Quickly, mistress of this tavern in the days of Sir John, and the liquor we were drinking, which seemed converted into sack and sugar.

"My dear Mrs. Quickly, cried I (for I knew her perfectly well at first sight) I am heartily glad to see you. How have you left Falstaff, Pistol, and the rest of our friends below stairs? brave and hearty, I hope?" "In good sooth, replied she, he did deserve to live for ever; but he maketh foul work on't where he hath flitted. Queen Proserpine and he have quarrelled for his attempting a rape upon her divinity; and were it not that she still had bowels of compassion, it more than seems probable, he might have been now sprawling in Tartarus."

I now found that spirits still preserve the frailties of the flesh; and that, according to the laws of criticism and dreaming, ghosts have been known to be guilty of even more than platonic affection: wherefore, as I found her too much moved on such a topic to proceed, I was resolved to change the subject; and desiring she would pledge me in a bumper, observed, with a sigh, that our sack was nothing now to what it was in former days: "Ah, Mrs. Quickly, those were merry times when you drew sack for prince Henry: men were twice as strong, and twice as wise, and much braver, and ten thousand times more charitable, than now. Those were the times! the battle of Agincourt was a victory indeed! Ever since that we have only been degenerating; and I have lived to see the day when drinking is no longer fashionable; when men wear clean shirts, and women shew their necks and arms. All are degenerated, Mrs. Quickly; and we shall probably, in another century, be frittered away into beaus or monkeys. Had you been on earth to see what I have seen, it would congeal all the blood in your body (your soul, I mean.) Why, our very nobility now have the intolerable arrogance, in spite of what is every day remonstrated from the press; our very nobility, I say, have the assurance to frequent assemblies, and presume to be as merry as the vulgar! See, my very friends have scarce manhood enough to sit to it till eleven, and I only am left to make a night on't. Pr'ythee do me the favour to console me a little for their absence by the story of your own adventure, or the history of the tavern where we are now sitting: I fancy the narrative may have something singular."

"Observe this apartment, interrupted my companion, of neat device and excellent workmanship—in this room I have lived, child, woman, and ghost, more than three hundred years: I am ordered by Pluto to keep an annual register of every transaction that passeth here; and I have whilom compiled three hundred tomes, which eftsoons may be submitted to thy regards." "None of your whiloms or eftsoons's, Mrs. Quickly, if you please, I replied: I know you can talk every whit as well as I can; for, as you have lived here so long, it is but natural to suppose you should learn the conversation of the company. Believe me, Dame, at best, you have neither too much sense or too much language to spare; so give me both as well as you can: but, first, my service to you: old women should water their clay a little now and then; and now to your story."

"The story of my own adventures, replied the vision, is but short and unsatisfactory; for, believe me, Mr. *Rigmarole*, believe me, a woman, with a butt of sack at her elbow, is never long-lived. Sir John's death afflicted me to such a degree, that I sincerely believe, to drown sorrow, I drank more liquor myself than I drew for my customers: my grief was sincere, and the sack was excellent. The prior of a neighbouring convent (for our priors then had as much power as a Middlesex justice now); he, I say, it was who gave me a licence for keeping a disorderly house; upon condition that I should never make hard bargains with the clergy; that he should have a bottle of sack every morning, and the liberty of confessing which of my girls he thought proper in private every night. I had continued for several years to pay this tribute; and he, it must be confessed, continued as rigorously to exact it. I grew old insensible: my customers continued however to compliment my looks while I was by; but I could hear them say I was wearing, when my back was turned. The prior, however, still was constant, and so were half his convent: but one fatal morning he missed the usual beverage; for I had incautiously drank over-night the last bottle myself. What will you have on't?—the very next day Doll Tearsheet and I were sent to the house of correction, and accused of keeping *a low bawdy-house*. In short, we were so well purified there with stripes, mortification, and penance, that we were afterwards utterly unfit for worldly conversation: though sack would have killed me, had I stuck to it, yet I soon died for want of a drop of something comfortable, and fairly left my body to the care of the beadle.

"Such is my own history; but that of the tavern, where I have ever since been stationed, affords greater variety. In the history of this, which is one of the oldest in London, you may view the different manners, pleasures, and follies of men at different periods. You will find mankind neither better nor worse now than formerly: the vices of an uncivilized people are generally more detestable, though not so frequent as those in polite society. It is the same luxury which formerly stuffed your alderman with plumb-porridge, and now crams him with turtle. It is the same low ambition that formerly induced a courtier to give up his religion to please his king, and now persuades him to give up his conscience to please his minister. It is the same vanity that formerly stained our ladies cheeks and necks with woad, and now paints them with carmine. Your ancient Briton formerly powdered his hair with red earth, like brick-dust, in order to appear frightful: your modern Briton cuts his hair on the crown, and plaisters it with hogs-lard and flour; and this to make him look killing. It is the same vanity, the same folly, and the same vice, only appearing different, as viewed through the glass of fashion. In a word, all mankind are a—"

"Sure the woman is dreaming, interrupted I. None of your reflections, Mrs. Quickly, if you love me; they only give me the spleen. Tell me your history at once.—I love stories, but hate reasoning."

"If you please then, Sir, returned my companion, I'll read you an abstract, which I made of the three hundred volumes I mentioned just now."

My body was no sooner laid in the dust, than the prior and several of his convent came to purify the tavern from the pollutions with which they said I had filled it. Masses were said in every room, reliques were exposed upon every piece of furniture, and the whole house washed with a deluge of holy water. My habitation was soon converted into a monastery; instead of customers now applying for sack and sugar, my rooms were crowded with images, reliques, saints, whores, and friars. Instead of being a scene of occasional debauchery, it was now filled with continual lewdness. The prior led the fashion, and the whole convent imitated his pious example. Matrons came hither to confess their sins, and to commit new. Virgins came hither, who seldom went virgins away. Nor was this a convent peculiarly wicked; every convent at that period was equally fond of pleasure, and gave a boundless loose to appetite. The laws allowed it; each priest had a right to a favourite companion, and a power of discarding her as often as he pleased. The laity grumbled, quarrelled with their wives and daughters, hated their confessors, and maintained them in opulence and ease. These, these were happy times, Mr. Rigmarole; these were times of piety, bravery, and simplicity! *Not so very happy, neither, good madam, pretty much like the present; those that labour starve, and those that do nothing wear fine cloaths, and live in luxury.*

In this manner, the fathers lived for some years without molestation; they transgressed, confessed themselves to each other, and were forgiven. One evening, however, our prior keeping a lady of distinction somewhat too long at confession, her husband unexpectedly came upon them, and testified all the indignation which was natural upon such an occasion. The prior assured the gentleman that it was the devil who had put it into his heart; and the lady was very very certain, that she was under the influence of magic, or she could never have behaved in so unfaithful a manner. The husband, however, was not to be put off by such evasion, but summoned both before the tribunal of justice. His proofs were flagrant; and he expected large damages. Such indeed he had a right to expect, were the tribunal of those days

constituted in the same manner as they are now. The cause
of the priest was to be tried before an assembly of priests;
and a layman was to expect redress only from their
impartiality and candour. What plea then do you think the
prior made to obviate this accusation? He denied the fact,
and challenged the plaintiff to try the merits of their cause by
single combat. It was a little hard, you may be sure, upon
the poor gentleman, not only to be made a cuckold, but to be
obliged to fight a duel into the bargain; yet such was the
justice of the times. The prior threw down his glove, and the
injured husband was obliged to take it up in token of his
accepting the challenge. Upon this the priest supplied his
champion, for it was not lawful for the clergy to fight; and
the defendant and plaintiff, according to custom, were put in
prison: both ordered to fast and pray, every method being
previously used to induce both to a confession of the truth.
After a month's imprisonment the hair of each was cut, the
bodies anointed with oil, the field of battle appointed and
guarded by soldiers, while his majesty presided over the
whole in person. Both the champions were sworn not to
seek victory either by fraud or magic. They prayed and
confessed upon their knees; and after these ceremonies, the
rest was left to the courage and conduct of the combatants.
As the champion, whom the prior had pitch'd upon, had
fought six or eight times upon similar occasions, it was no
way extraordinary to find him victorious in the present
combat. In short, the husband was discomfited, he was
taken from the field of battle, stripp'd to his shirt; and, after
one of his legs was cut off, as justice ordained in such cases,
he was hanged as a terror to future offenders. These, these
were the times, Mr. Rigmarole; you see how much more
just, and wise, and valiant our ancestors were than us. *I
rather fancy, madam, that the times then were pretty much
like our own; where a multiplicty of laws give a judge as*

much power as a want of law, since he is ever sure to find
among the number some to countenance his partiality.

Our convent, victorious over their enemies, now gave a
loose to every demonstration of joy. The lady became a nun,
the prior was made a bishop, and three Wickliffites were
burned in the illuminations and fire-works that were made on
the present occasion. Our convent now began to enjoy a very
high degree of reputation. There was not one in London that
had the character of hating heretics to much as ours. Ladies
of the first distinction chose from our convent their
confessors; in short, it flourished, and might have flourished
to this hour, but for a fatal accident which terminated in its
overthrow. The lady whom the prior had placed in a
nunnery, and whom he continued to visit for some times
with great punctuality, began at last to perceive that she was
quite forsaken. Secluded from conversation as usual, she
now entertained the visions of a devotee; found herself
strangely disturbed; but hesitated in determining, whether
she was possessed by an angel or a dæmon. She was not
long in suspense; for, upon vomiting a large quantity of
crooked pins, and finding the palms of her hands turned
outwards, she quickly concluded that she was possessed by
the devil. She soon lost entirely the use of speech; and when
she seemed to speak, every body that was present perceived
that the voice was not her own, but that of the devil within
her. In short, she was bewitched; and all the difficulty lay in
determining who it could be that bewitched her. The nuns
and the monks all demanded the magician's name, but the
devil made no reply; for he knew they had no authority to
ask questions. By the rules of witchcraft, when an evil spirit
has taken possession, he may refuse to answer any
questions asked him, unless they are put by a bishop, and to
these he is obliged to reply. A bishop, therefore, was sent
for, and now the whole secret came out: the devil reluctantly

owned that he was a servant of the prior; that by his command he resided in his present habitation; and that without his command he was resolved to keep in possession. The bishop was an able exorcist; he drove the devil out by force of mystical arms; the prior was arraigned for witchcraft; the witnesses were strong and numerous against him, not less than fourteen persons being by, who heard the devil talk Latin. There was no resisting such a cloud of witnesses, the prior was condemned; and he who had assisted at so many burnings, was burned himself in turn. These were the times, Mr. Rigmarole; the people of those times were not infidels as now, but sincere believers! *Equally faulty with ourselves; they believed what the devil was pleased to tell them; and we seem resolved, at last, to believe neither God nor devil.*

After such a stain upon the convent, it was not to be supposed it could subsist any longer; the fathers were ordered to decamp, and the house was once again converted into a tavern. The king conferred it on one of his cast mistresses; she was constituted landlady by royal authority; and as the tavern was in the neighbourhood of the court, and the mistress a very polite woman, it began to have more business than ever; and sometimes took not less than four shillings a day.

But perhaps you are desirous of knowing what were the peculiar qualifications of women of fashion at that period; and in a description of the present landlady, you will have a tolerable idea of all the rest. This lady was the daughter of a nobleman, and received such an education in the country as became her quality, beauty, and great expectations. She could make shifts and hose for herself and all the servants of the family, when she was twelve years old. She knew the names of the four and twenty letters, so that it was impossible to bewitch her; and this was a greater piece of learning, than any lady in the whole country could pretend to. She was always up early; and saw breakfast served in the great hall by six o'clock. At this scene of festivity she generally improved good humour, by telling her dreams, relating stories of spirits, several of which she herself had seen; and one of which she was reported to have killed with a black-hafted knife. From hence she usually went to make pastry in the larder, and here she was followed by her sweet-hearts, who were much helped on in conversation by struggling with her for kisses. About ten, miss generally went to play at hot-cockles and blindman's buff, in the parlour; and when the young folks (for they seldom played at hot-cockles when grown old) were tired of such amusements, the gentlemen entertained miss with the history of their greyhounds, bear-baitings, and victories at cudgel-playing. If the weather was fine they ran at the ring, shot at butts, while miss held in her hand a ribbon, with which she adorned the conqueror. Her mental qualifications were exactly fitted to her external accomplishments. Before she was fifteen she could tell the story of Jack the Giant Killer, could name every mountain that was inhabited by fairies, knew a witch at first sight, and could repeat four Latin prayers without a prompter. Her dress was perfectly fashionable; her arms and her hair were completely covered; a monstrous ruff was put round her neck; so that her head seemed like that of John the Baptist placed in a charger. In short, when completely equipped, her appearance was so very modest, that she discovered little more than her nose. These were the times, Mr. Rigmarole; when every lady that had a good nose, might set up for a beauty; when every woman that could tell stories, might be cried up for a wit. *I am as much displeased at those dresses which conceal too much, as at those which discover too much: I am equally an enemy to a female dunce or a female pedant.*

You may be sure that miss chose an husband with qualifications resembling her own; she pitched upon a courtier, equally remarkable for hunting and drinking, who had given several proofs of his great virility among the daughters of his tenants and domestics. They fell in love at first sight, for such was the gallantry of the times, were married, came to court, and madam appeared with superior qualifications. The king was struck with her beauty. All property was at the king's command, the husband was obliged to resign all pretensions in his wife to the sovereign whom God had anointed, to commit adultery where he thought proper. The king loved her for some time, but at length repenting of his misdeeds, and instigated by his father confessor, from a principle of conscience removed her from his levee to the bar of this tavern, and took a new mistress in her stead. Let it not surprize you to behold the mistress of a king degraded to so humble an office. As the ladies had no mental accomplishments, a good face was enough to raise them to the royal couch; and she who was this day a royal mistress, might the next, when her beauty palled upon enjoyment, be doomed to infamy and want.

Under the care of this lady the tavern grew into great reputation; the courtiers had not yet learned to game, but they paid it off by drinking; drunkenness is ever the vice of a barbarous, and gaming of a luxurious age. They had not such frequent entertainments as the moderns have, but were more expensive and more luxurious in those they had. All their fooleries were more elaborate, and more admired by the great and the vulgar than now. A courtier has been known to spend his whole fortune at a single feast, a king to mortgage his dominions to furnish out the fripery of a tournament. There were certain days appointed for riot and debauchery, and to be sober at such times was reputed a crime. Kings themselves set the example; and I have seen monarchs in this room drunk before the entertainment was half concluded. *These were the times, sir, when kings kept mistresses, and got drunk in public; they were too plain and simple in those happy times to hide their vices, and act the hypocrite as now.* Lord! Mrs. Quickly, interrupting her, I expected to have heard a story, and here you are going to tell me I know not what of times, and vices; prithee, let me intreat thee once more to wave reflections, and give thy history without deviation.

No lady upon earth, continued my visionary correspondent, knew how to put off her damaged wine or women with more art than she. When these grew flat or those paltry, it was but changing the names; the wine became excellent, and the girls agreeable. She was also possessed of the engaging leer, the chuck under the chin, winked at a double entendre, could nick the opportunity of calling for something comfortable; and perfectly understood the discreet moments when to withdraw. The gallants of those times pretty much resembled the bloods of ours; they were fond of pleasure, but quite ignorant of the art of refining upon it: thus a court bawd of those times resembled the common low-lived harridan of a modern bagnio. Witness, ye powers of debauchery, how often I have been present at the various appearances of drunkenness, riot, guilt, and brutality? a tavern is a true picture of human infirmity, in history we find only one side of the age exhibited to our view, but in the accounts of a tavern we see every age equally absurd and equally vicious.

Upon this lady's decease the tavern was successively occupied by adventurers, bullies, pimps, and gamesters. Towards the conclusion of the reign of Henry VII, gaming was more universally practised in England than even now. Kings themselves have been known to play off, at Primero, not only all the money and jewels they could part with, but the very images in churches. The last Henry played away, in this very room, not only the four great bells of St. Paul's cathedral, but the fine image of St. Paul, which stood upon the top of the spire, to Sir Miles Partridge, who took them down the next day, and sold them by auction. Have you, then, any cause to regret being born in the times you now live? or do you still believe that human nature continues to run on declining every age? If we observe the actions of the busy part of mankind, your ancestors will be found infinitely more gross, servile, and even dishonest, than you. If, forsaking history, we only trace them in their hours of amusement and dissipation, we shall find them more sensual, more entirely devoted to pleasure, and infinitely more selfish.

The last hostess of note I find upon record was Jane Rouse. She was born among the lower ranks of the people; and by frugality, and extreme complaisance, contrived to acquire a moderate fortune: this she might have enjoyed for many years, had she not unfortunately quarrelled with one of her neighbours, a woman who was in high repute for sanctity thro' the whole parish. In the times of which I speak, two women seldom quarrelled, that one did not accuse the other of witchcraft, and she who first contrived to vomit crooked pins was sure to come off victorious. The scandal of a modern tea-table differs widely from the scandal of former times: the fascination of a lady's eyes, at present, is regarded as a compliment; but if a lady, formerly, should be accused of having witchcraft in her eyes, it were much better, both for her soul and body, that she had no eyes at all.

In short, Jane Rouse was accused of witchcraft: and, though she made the best defence she could, it was all to no purpose; she was taken from her own bar to the bar of the Old Bailey, condemned, and executed accordingly. These were times indeed! when even women could not scold in safety. Since her time the tavern underwent several revolutions, according to the spirit of the times, or the disposition of the reigning monarch. It was this day a brothel, and the next a conventicle for enthusiasts. It was one year noted for harbouring whigs, and the next infamous for a retreat to tories. Some years ago it was in high vogue, but at present it seems declining. This only may be remarked in general, that whenever taverns flourish most, the times are then most extravagant and luxurious. Lord! Mrs. Quickly, interrupted I, you have really deceived me; I expected a romance, and here you have been this half hour giving me only a description of the spirit of the times: if you have nothing but tedious remarks to communicate, seek some other hearer: I am determined to hearken only to stories. I had scarce concluded, when my eyes and ears seemed opened to my landlord, who had been all this while giving me an account of the repairs he had made in the house; and was not got into the story of the crack'd glass in the dining-room.

STRATFORD-ON-AVON

Washington Irving

Thou soft-flowing Avon, by thy silver stream
Of things more than mortal sweet Shakspeare would dream;
The fairies by moonlight dance round his green bed,
For hallow'd the turf is which pillow'd his head.

GARRICK

To a homeless man, who has no spot on this wide world
which he can truly call his own, there is a momentary feeling
of something like independence and territorial consequence,
when, after a weary day's travel, he kicks off his boots,
thrusts his feet into slippers, and stretches himself before an
inn fire. Let the world without go as it may; let kingdoms
rise or fall, so long as he has the wherewithal to pay his bill,
he is, for the time being, the very monarch of all he surveys.
The arm-chair is his throne, the poker his sceptre, and the
little parlor, some twelve feet square, his undisputed empire.
It is a morsel of certainty, snatched from the midst of the
uncertainties of life; it is a sunny moment gleaming out

kindly on a cloudy day; and he who had advanced some way on a pilgrimage of existence, knows the importance of husbanding even morsels and moments of enjoyment. "Shall I not take mine ease in mine inn?" thought I, as I gave the fire a stir, lolled back in my elbow-chair, and cast a complacent look about the little parlor of the Red Horse, at Stratford-on-Avon.

The words of sweet Shakspeare were just passing through my mind as the clock struck midnight from the tower of the church in which he lies buried. There was a gentle tap at the door, and a pretty chambermaid, putting in her smiling face, inquired, with a hesitating air, whether I had rung. I understood it as a modest hint that it was time to retire. My dream of absolute dominion was at an end; so abdicating my throne, like a prudent potentate, to avoid being deposed, and putting the Stratford Guide-Book under my arm, as a pillow companion, I went to bed, and dreamt all night of Shakspeare, the jubilee, and David Garrick.

The next morning was one of those quickening mornings which we sometimes have in early spring; for it was about the middle of March. The chills of a long winter had suddenly given way; the north wind had spent its last gasp; and a mild air came stealing from the west, breathing the breath of life into nature, and wooing every bud and flower to burst forth into fragrance and beauty.

I had come to Stratford on a poetical pilgrimage. My first visit was to the house where Shakspeare was born, and where, according to tradition, he was brought up to his father's craft of wool-combing. It is a small, mean-looking edifice of wood and plaster, a true nestling-place of genius, which seems to delight in hatching its offspring in by-corners. The walls of its squalid chambers are covered with names and inscriptions in every language, by pilgrims of all nations, ranks, and conditions, from the prince to the peasant; and present a simple, but striking instance of the spontaneous and universal homage of mankind to the great poet of nature.

The house is shown by a garrulous old lady, in a frosty red face, lighted up by a cold blue anxious eye, and garnished with artificial locks of flaxen hair, curling from under an exceedingly dirty cap. She was peculiarly assiduous in exhibiting the relics with which this, like all other celebrated shrines, abounds. There was the shattered stock of the very matchlock with which Shakspeare shot the deer, on his poaching exploits. There, too, was his tobacco-box; which proves that he was a rival smoker of Sir Walter Raleigh; the sword also with which he played Hamlet; and the identical lantern with which Friar Laurence discovered Romeo and Juliet at the tomb! There was an ample supply also of Shakspeare's mulberry-tree, which seems to have as extraordinary powers of self-multiplication as the wood of the true cross; of which there is enough extant to build a ship of the line.

The most favorite object of curiosity, however, is Shakspeare's chair. It stands in the chimney nook of a small gloomy chamber, just behind what was his father's shop. Here he may many a time have sat when a boy, watching the slowly revolving spit with all the longing of an urchin; or of an evening, listening to the cronies and gossips of Stratford, dealing forth churchyard tales and legendary anecdotes of the troublesome times of England. In this chair it is the custom of every one that visits the house to sit: whether this be done with the hope of imbibing any of the inspiration of the bard I am at a loss to say, I merely mention the fact; and mine hostess privately assured me, that, though built of solid oak, such was the fervent zeal of devotees, that the chair had to be new bottomed at least once in three years. It is worthy of notice also, in the history of this extraordinary chair, that it

partakes something of the volatile nature of the Santa Casa of
Loretto, or the flying chair of the Arabian enchanter; for
though sold some few years since to a northern princess,
yet, strange to tell, it has found its way back again to the old
chimney corner.

I am always of easy faith in such matters, and am ever
willing to be deceived, where the deceit is pleasant and costs
nothing. I am therefore a ready believer in relics, legends,
and local anecdotes of goblins and great men; and would
advise all travellers who travel for their gratification to be the
same. What is it to us, whether these stories be true or false,
so long as we can persuade ourselves into the belief of them,
and enjoy all the charm of the reality? There is nothing like
resolute good-humored credulity in these matters; and on this
occasion I went even so far as willingly to believe the claims
of mine hostess to a lineal descent from the poet, when,
luckily for my faith, she put into my hands a play of her own
composition, which set all belief in her consanguinity at
defiance.

From the birthplace of Shakspeare a few paces brought
me to his grave. He lies buried in the chancel of the parish
church, a large and venerable pile, mouldering with age, but
richly ornamented. It stands on the banks of the Avon, on an
embowered point, and separated by adjoining gardens from
the suburbs of the town. Its situation is quiet and retired; the
river runs murmuring at the foot of the churchyard, and the
elms which grow upon its banks droop their branches into
its clear bosom. An avenue of limes, the boughs of which
are curiously interlaced, so as to form in summer an arched
way of foliage, leads up from the gate of the yard to the
church-porch. The graves are overgrown with grass; the
gray tombstones, some of them nearly sunk into the earth,
are half covered with moss, which has likewise tinted the
reverend old building. Small birds have built their nests

among the cornices and fissures of the walls, and keep up a continual flutter and chirping; and rooks are sailing and cawing about its lofty gray spire.

In the course of my rambles I met with the gray-headed sexton, Edmonds, and accompanied him home to get the key of the church. He had lived in Stratford, man and boy, for eighty years, and seemed still to consider himself a vigorous man, with the trivial exception that he had nearly lost the use of his legs for a few years past. His dwelling was a cottage, looking out upon the Avon and its bordering meadows; and was a picture of that neatness, order, and comfort, which pervade the humblest dwellings in this country. A low white-washed room, with a stone floor carefully scrubbed, served for parlor, kitchen, and hall. Rows of pewter and earthen dishes glittered along the dresser. On an old oaken table, well rubbed and polished, lay the family Bible and prayer-book, and the drawer contained the family library, composed of about half a score of well-thumbed volumes. An ancient clock, that important article of cottage furniture, ticked on the opposite side of the room; with a bright warming-pan hanging on one side of it, and the old man's horn-handled Sunday cane on the other. The fireplace, as usual, was wide and deep enough to admit a gossip knot within its jambs. In one corner sat the old man's granddaughter sewing, a pretty blue-eyed girl,—and in the opposite corner was a superannuated crony, whom he addressed by the name of John Ange, and who, I found, had been his companion from childhood. They had played together in infancy; they had worked together in manhood; they were now tottering about and gossiping away the evening of life; and in a short time they will probably be buried together in the neighboring churchyard. It is not often that we see two streams of existence running thus evenly and tranquilly side by side; it is only in such quite "bosom scenes" of life that they are to be met with.

I had hoped to gather some traditionary anecdotes of the bard from these ancient chroniclers; but they had nothing new to impart. The long interval during which Shakspeare's writing lay in comparative neglect has spread its shadow over his history; and it is his good or evil lot that scarcely anything remains to his biographers but a scanty handful of conjectures.

The sexton and his companion had been employed as carpenters on the preparations for the celebrated Stratford jubilee, and they remembered Garrick, the prime mover of the fête, who superintended the arrangements, and who, according to the sexton, was "a short punch man, very lively and bustling." John Ange had assisted also in cutting down Shakspeare's mulberry-tree, of which he had a morsel in his pocket for sale; no doubt a sovereign quickener of literary conception.

I was grieved to hear these two worthy wights speak very dubiously of the eloquent dame who shows the Shakspeare house. John Ange shook his head when I mentioned her valuable collection of relics, particularly her remains of the mulberry-tree; and the old sexton even expressed a doubt as to Shakspeare having been born in her house. I soon discovered that he looked upon her mansion with an evil eye, as a rival to the poet's tomb; the latter having comparatively but few visitors. Thus it is that historians differ at the very outset, and mere pebbles make the stream of truth diverge into different channels even at the fountain-head.

We approached the church through the avenue of limes, and entered by a Gothic porch, highly ornamented, with carved doors of massive oak. The interior is spacious, and the architecture and embellishments superior to those of most country churches. There are several ancient monuments of nobility and gentry, over some of which hang funeral escutcheons, and banners dropping piecemeal from the walls. The tomb of Shakspeare is in the chancel. The place is solemn and sepulchral. Tall elms wave before the pointed windows, and the Avon, which runs at a short distance from the walls, keeps up a low perpetual murmur. A flat stone marks the spot where the bard is buried. There are four lines inscribed on it, said to have been written by himself, and which have in them something extremely awful. If they are indeed his own, they show that solicitude about the quiet of the grave, which seems natural to fine sensibilities and thoughtful minds.

> Good friend, for Jesus' sake forbeare
> To dig the dust enclosed here.
> Blessed be he that spares these stones,
> And curst be he that moves my bones.

Just over the grave, in a niche of the wall, is a bust of Shakspeare, put up shortly after his death, and considered as a resemblance. The aspect is pleasant and serene, with a finely arched forehead, and I thought I could read in it clear indications of that cheerful, social disposition, by which he was as much characterized among his contemporaries as by the vastness of his genius. The inscription mentions his age at the time of his decease—fifty-three years; an untimely death for the world: for what fruit might not have been expected from the golden autumn of such a mind, sheltered as it was from the stormy vicissitudes of life, and flourishing in the sunshine of popular and royal favor.

The inscription on the tombstone has not been without its effect. It has prevented the removal of his remains from the bosom of his native place to Westminster Abbey, which was at one time contemplated. A few years since also, as some laborers were digging to make an adjoining vault, the earth caved in, so as to leave a vacant space almost like an arch, through which one might have reached into his grave. No one, however, presumed to meddle with his remains so awfully guarded by a malediction; and lest any of the idle or the curious, or any collector of relics, should be tempted to commit depredations, the old sexton kept watch over the place for two days, until the vault was finished and the aperture closed again. He told me that he had made bold to look in at the hole, but could see neither coffin nor bones; nothing but dust. It was something, I thought, to have seen the dust of Shakspeare.

Next to this grave are those of his wife, his favorite daughter, Mrs. Hall, and others of his family. On a tomb close by, also, is a full-length effigy of his old friend John Combe of usurious memory; on whom he is said to have written a ludicrous epitaph. There are other monuments around, but the mind refuses to dwell on anything that is not connected with Shakspeare. His idea pervades the place; the whole pile seems but as his mausoleum. The feelings, no longer checked and thwarted by doubt, here indulge in perfect confidence: other traces of him may be false or dubious, but here is palpable evidence and absolute certainty. As I trod the sounding pavement, there was something intense and thrilling in the idea that, in very truth, the remains of Shakspeare were mouldering beneath my feet. It was a long time before I could prevail upon myself to leave the place; and as I passed through the churchyard, I plucked a branch from one of the yew-trees, the only relic that I have brought from Stratford.

I had now visited the usual objects of a pilgrim's devotion, but I had a desire to see the old family seat of the Lucys, at Charlecot, and to ramble through the park where

Shakspeare, in company with some of the roysters of Stratford, committed his youthful offence of deer-stealing. In this hare-brained exploit we are told that he was taken prisoner, and carried to the keeper's lodge, where he remained all night in doleful captivity. When brought into the presence of Sir Thomas Lucy, his treatment must have been galling and humiliating; for it so wrought upon his spirit as to produce a rough pasquinade, which was affixed to the park gate at Charlecot.[1]

This flagitious attack upon the dignity of the knight so incensed him, that he applied to a lawyer at Warwick to put the severity of the laws in force against the rhyming deer-stalker. Shakspeare did not wait to brave the united puissance of a knight of the shire and a country attorney. He forthwith abandoned the pleasant banks of the Avon and his paternal trade; wandered away to London; became a hanger-on to the theatres; then an actor; and, finally, wrote for the stage; and thus, through the persecution of Sir Thomas Lucy, Stratford lost an indifferent wool-comber, and the world gained an immortal poet. He retained, however, for a long time, a sense of the harsh treatment of the Lord of Charlecot, and revenged himself in his writings; but in the sportive way of a good-natured mind. Sir Thomas is said to be the original Justice Shallow, and the satire is slyly fixed upon him by the justice's armorial bearings, which, like those of the knight, had white luces[2] in the quarterlings.

Various attempts have been made by his biographers to soften and explain away this early transgression of the poet; but I look upon it as one of those thoughtless exploits natural to his situation and turn of mind. Shakspeare, when young, had doubtless all the wildness and irregularity of an ardent, undisciplined, and undirected genius. The poetic temperament has naturally something in it the vagabond. When left to itself it runs loosely and wildly, and delights in

everything eccentric and licentious. It is often a turn-up of a
die, in the gambling freaks of fate, whether a natural genius
shall turn out a great rogue or a great poet; and had not
Shakspeare's mind fortunately taken a literary bias, he might
have as daringly transcended all civil, as he has all dramatic
laws.

I have little doubt that, in early life, when running, like
an unbroken colt, about the neighborhood of Stratford, he
was to be found in the company of all kinds of odd
anomalous characters; that he associated with all the madcaps
of the place, and was one of those unlucky urchins, at
mention of whom old men shake their heads, and predict that
they will one day come to the gallows. To him the poaching
in Sir Thomas Lucy's park was doubtless like a foray to a
Scottish knight, and struck his eager, and, as yet untamed,
imagination, as something delightfully adventurous.[3]

The old mansion of Charlecot and its surrounding park
still remain in the possession of the Lucy family, and are
peculiarly interesting, from being connected with this
whimsical but eventful circumstance in the scanty history of
the bard. As the house stood but little more than three miles'
distance from Stratford, I resolved to pay it a pedestrian
visit, that I might stroll leisurely through some of those
scenes from which Shakspeare must have derived his earliest
ideas of rural imagery.

The country was yet naked and leafless; but English
scenery is always verdant, and the sudden change in the
temperature of the weather was surprising in its quickening
effects upon the landscape. It was inspiring and animating to
witness this first awakening of spring; to feel its warm
breath stealing over the senses; to see the moist mellow earth
beginning to put forth the green sprout and the tender blade;
and the trees and shrubs, in their reviving tints and bursting
buds, giving the promise of returning foliage and flower.

The cold snowdrop, that little borderer on the skirts of winter, was to be seen with its chaste white blossoms in the small gardens before the cottages. The bleating of the new-dropt lambs was faintly heard from the fields. The sparrow twittered about the thatched eaves and budding hedges; the robin threw a livelier note into his late querulous wintry strain; and the lark, springing up from the reeking bosom of the meadow, towered away into the bright fleecy cloud, pouring forth torrents of melody. As I watched the little songster, mounting up higher and higher, until his body was a mere speck on the white bosom of the cloud, while the ear was still filled with his music, it called to mind Shakspeare's exquisite little song in Cymbeline:—

Hark! hark! the lark at heaven's gate sings,
    And Phœbus 'gins arise,
His steeds to water at those springs,
    On chaliced flowers that lies.

And winking mary-buds begin
    To ope their golden eyes;
With everything that pretty bin,
    My lady sweet, arise!

Indeed the whole country about here is poetic ground: everything is associated with the idea of Shakspeare. Every old cottage that I saw, I fancied into some resort of his boyhood, where he had acquired his intimate knowledge of rustic life and manners, and heard those legendary tales and wild superstitions which he has woven like witchcraft into his dramas. For in his time, we are told, it was a popular amusement in winter evenings "to sit round the fire, and tell merry tales of errant knights, queens, lovers, lords, ladies, giants, dwarfs, thieves, cheaters, witches, fairies, goblins, and friars."[4]

My route for a part of the way lay in sight of the Avon, which made a variety of the most fancy doublings and windings through a wide and fertile valley; sometimes glittering from among willows, which fringed its borders; sometimes disappearing among groves, or beneath green banks; and sometimes rambling out into full view, and making an azure sweep round a slope of meadow land. This beautiful bosom of country is called the Vale of the Red Horse. A distant line of undulating blue hills seems to be its boundary, whilst all the soft intervening landscape lies in a manner enchained in the silver links of the Avon.

After pursuing the road for about three miles, I turned off into a footpath, which led along the borders of fields, and under hedgerows to a private gate of the park; there was a stile, however, for the benefit of the pedestrian; there being a public right of way through the grounds. I delight in these hospitable estates, in which every one has a kind of property—at least as far as the footpath is concerned. It in some measure reconciles a poor man to his lot, and, what is more, to the better lot of his neighbor, thus to have parks and pleasure-grounds thrown open for his recreation. He breathes the pure air as freely, and lolls as luxuriously under the shade, as the lord of the soil; and if he has not the privilege of calling all that he sees his own, he has not, at the same time, the trouble of paying for it, and keeping it in order.

I now found myself among noble avenues of oaks and elms, whose vast size bespoke the growth of centuries. The wind sounded solemnly among their branches, and the rooks cawed from their hereditary nests in the tree-tops. The eye ranged through a long lessening vista, with nothing to interrupt the view but a distant statue; and a vagrant deer stalking like a shadow across the opening.

There is something about these stately old avenues that has the effect of Gothic architecture, not merely from the pretended similarity of form, but from their bearing the evidence of long duration, and of having had their origin in a period of time with which we associate ideas of romantic grandeur. They betoken also the long-settled dignity, and proudly concentrated independence of an ancient family; and I have heard a worthy but aristocratic old friend observe, when speaking of the sumptuous palaces of modern gentry, that "money could do much with stone and mortar, but, thank Heaven, there was no such thing as suddenly building up an avenue of oaks."

It was from wandering in early life among this rich scenery, and about the romantic solitudes of the adjoining part of Fullbroke, which then formed a part of the Lucy estate, that some of Shakspeare's commentators have supposed he derived his noble forest meditations of Jaques, and the enchanting woodland pictures in "As You Like It." It is in lonely wanderings through such scenes, that the mind drinks deep but quiet draughts of inspiration, and becomes intensely sensible of the beauty and majesty of nature. The imagination kindles into revery and rapture; vague but exquisite images and ideas keep breaking upon it; and we revel in a mute and almost incommunicable luxury of thought. It was in some such mood, and perhaps under one of those very trees before me, which threw their broad shades over the grassy banks and quivering waters of the Avon, that the poet's fancy may have sallied forth into that little song which breathes the very soul of a rural voluptuary.

> Under the green wood tree,
> Who loves to lie with me,
> And tune his merry throat
> Unto the sweet bird's note,

Come hither, come hither, come hither.
        Here shall he see
        No enemy,
But winter and rough weather.

I had now come in sight of the house. It is a large building of brick, with stone quoins, and is in the Gothic style of Queen Elizabeth's day, having been built in the first year of her reign. The exterior remains very nearly in its original state, and may be considered a fair specimen of the residence of a wealthy country gentleman of those days. A great gateway opens from the park into a kind of courtyard in front of the house, ornamented with a grass-plot, shrubs, and flower-beds. The gateway is in imitation of the ancient barbican; being a kind of outpost, and flanked by towers; though evidently for mere ornament, instead of defence. The front of the house is completely in the old style; with stone-shafted casements, a great bow-window of heavy stone-work, and a portal with armorial bearings over it, carved in stone. At each corner of the building is an octagon tower, surmounted by a gilt ball and weathercock.

The Avon, which winds through the park, makes a bend just at the foot of a gently sloping bank, which sweeps down from the rear of the house. Large herds of deer were feeding or reposing upon its borders; and swans were sailing majestically upon its bosom. As I contemplated the venerable old mansion, I called to mind Falstaff's encomium on Justice Shallow's abode, and the affected indifference and real vanity of the latter.

Falstaff. You have a goodly dwelling and a rich.
Shallow. Barren, barren, barren; beggars all, beggars all, Sir John:—marry, good air.

Whatever may have been the joviality of the old mansion in the days of Shakspeare, it had now an air of stillness and solitude. The great iron gateway that opened into the courtyard was locked; there was no show of servants bustling about the place; the deer gazed quietly at me as I passed, being no longer harried by the moss-troopers of Stratford. The only sign of domestic life that I met with was a white cat, stealing with wary look and stealthy pace towards the stables, as if on some nefarious expedition. I must not omit to mention the carcass of a scoundrel crow which I saw suspended against the barn wall, as it shows that the Lucys still inherit that lordly abhorrence of poachers, and maintain that rigorous exercise of territorial power which was so strenuously manifested in the case of the bard.

After prowling about for some time, I at length found my way to a lateral portal, which was the everyday entrance to the mansion. I was courteously received by a worthy old housekeeper, who, with the civility and communicativeness of her order, showed me the interior of the house. The greater part has undergone alterations, and been adapted to modern tastes and modes of living: there is a fine old oaken staircase; and the great hall, that noble feature in an ancient manor-house, still retains much of the appearance it must have had in the days of Shakspeare. The ceiling is arched and lofty; and at one end is a gallery in which stands an organ. The weapons and trophies of the chase, which formerly adorned the hall of a country gentleman, have made way for family portraits. There is a wide hospitable fireplace, calculated for an ample old-fashioned wood fire, formerly the rallying-place of winter festivity. On the opposite side of the hall is the huge Gothic bow-window, with stone shafts, which looks out upon the courtyard. Here are emblazoned in stained glass the armorial bearings of the Lucy family for many generations, some being dated in

1558. I was delighted to observe in the quarterings the three *white luces*, by which the character of Sir Thomas was first identified with that of Justice Shallow. They are mentioned in the first scene of the "Merry Wives of Windsor," where the Justice is in a rage with Falstaff for having "beaten his men, killed his deer, and broken into his lodge." The poet had no doubt the offences of himself and his comrades in mind at the time, and we may suppose the family pride and vindictive threats of the puissant Shallow to be a caricature of the pompous indignation of Sir Thomas.

Shallow. Sir Hugh, persuade me not; I will make a Star-Chamber matter of it; if he were twenty John Falstaffs, he shall not abuse Sir Robert Shallow, Esq.
Slender. In the county of Gloster, justice of peace, and *coram.*
Shallow. Ay, cousin Slender, and *custalorum.*
Slender. Ay, and *ratalorum* too, and a gentleman born, master parson; who writes himself *Armigero* in any bill, warrant, quittance, or obligation, *Armigero.*
Shallow. Ay, that I do; and have done any time these three hundred years.
Slender. All his successors gone before him have done 't, and all his ancestors that come after him may; they may give the dozen *white luces* in their coat. . . .
Shallow. The council shall hear it; it is a riot.
Evans. It is not meet the council hear of a riot; there is no fear of Got in a riot; the council, hear you, shall desire to hear the fear of Got, and not to hear a riot; take your vizaments in that.
Shallow. Ha! o' my life, if I were young again, the sword should end it!

Near the window thus emblazoned hung a portrait by Sir Peter Lely, of one of the Lucy family, a great beauty of the time of Charles the Second: the old housekeeper shook her head as she pointed to the picture, and informed me that this lady had been sadly addicted to cards, and had gambled away a great portion of the family estate, among which was that part of the park where Shakspeare and his comrades had killed the deer. The lands thus lost had not been entirely regained by the family even at the present day. It is but justice to this recreant dame to confess that she had a surpassingly fine hand and arm.

The picture which most attracted my attention was a great painting over the fireplace, containing likenesses of Sir Thomas Lucy and his family, who inhabited the hall in the latter part of Shakspeare's lifetime. I at first thought that it was the vindictive knight himself, but the housekeeper assured me that it was his son; the only likeness extant of the former being an effigy upon his tomb in the church of the neighboring hamlet of Charlecot.[5] The picture gives a lively idea of the costume and manners of the time. Sir Thomas is dressed in ruff and doublet; white shoes with roses in them; and has a peaked yellow, or, as Master Slender would say, "a cane-colored beard." His lady is seated on the opposite side of the picture, in wide ruff and long stomacher, and the children have a most venerable stiffness and formality of dress. Hounds and spaniels are mingled in the family group; a hawk is seated on his perch in the foreground, and one of the children holds a bow;—all intimating the knight's skill in hunting, hawking, and archery—so indispensable to an accomplished gentleman in those days.[6]

I regretted to find that the ancient furniture of the hall had disappeared; for I had hoped to meet with the stately elbow-chair of carved oak, in which the country squire of former days was wont to sway the sceptre of empire over his rural domains; and in which it might be presumed the redoubted Sir Thomas sat enthroned in awful state when the recreant Shakspeare was brought before him. As I like to deck out pictures for my own entertainment, I pleased myself with the idea that this very hall had been the scene of the unlucky bard's examination on the morning after his captivity in the lodge. I fancied to myself the rural potentate, surrounded by his body-guard of butler, pages, and blue-coated serving-men, with their badges; while the luckless culprit was brought in, forlorn and chopfallen in the custody of gamekeepers, huntsmen, and whippers-in, and followed by a rabble rout of country clowns. I fancied bright faces of curious housemaids peeping from the half-opened doors; while from the gallery the fair daughters of the knight leaned gracefully forward, eyeing the youthful prisoner with that pity "that dwells in womanhood."—Who would have thought that this poor varlet, thus trembling before the brief authority of a country squire, and the sport of rustic boors, was soon to become the delight of princes, the theme of all tongues and ages, the dictator to the human mind, and was to confer immortality on his oppressor by a caricature and a lampoon!

I was now invited by the butler to walk into the garden, and I felt inclined to visit the orchard and arbor where the justice treated Sir John Falstaff and Cousin Silence "to a last year's pippin of his own grafting, with a dish of caraways"; but I had already spent so much of the day in my ramblings that I was obliged to give up any further investigations. When about to take my leave I was gratified by the civil entreaties of the housekeeper and butler, that I would take some refreshment: an instance of good old hospitality which, I grieve to say, we castle-hunters seldom meet with in modern days. I make no doubt it is a virtue which the present representative of the Lucys inherits from his ancestors; for Shakspeare, even in his caricature, makes Justice Shallow importunate in this respect, as witness his pressing instances to Falstaff.

By cock and pye, sir, you shall not away to-night. . . . I will not excuse you; you shall not be excused; excuses shall not be admitted; there is no excuse shall serve; you shall not be excused. . . . Some pigeons, Davy; a couple of short-legged hens; a joint of mutton; and any pretty little tiny kickshaws, tell William Cook.

I now bade a reluctant farewell to the old hall. My mind had become so completely possessed by the imaginary scenes and characters connected with it, that I seemed to be actually living among them. Everything brought them as it were before my eyes; and as the door of the dining-room opened, I almost expected to hear the feeble voice of Master Silence quavering forth his favorite ditty:—

'T is merry in hall, when beards wag all,
And welcome merry shrove-tide!

On returning to my inn, I could not but reflect on the singular gift of the poet; to be able thus to spread the magic of his mind over the very face of nature; to give to things and places a charm and character not their own, and to turn this "working-day world" into a perfect fairyland. He is indeed the true enchanter, whose spell operates, not upon the senses, but upon the imagination and the heart. Under the wizard influence of Shakspeare I had been walking all day in a complete delusion. I had surveyed the landscape through the prism of poetry, which tinged every object with the hues of the rainbow. I had been surrounded with fancied beings; with mere airy nothings, conjured up by poetic power; yet which, to me, had all the charm of reality. I had heard Jaques soliloquize beneath his oak: had beheld the fair Rosalind and her companion adventuring through the woodlands; and, above all, had been once more present in spirit with fat Jack Falstaff and his contemporaries, from the august Justice Shallow, down to the gentle Master Slender and the sweet Anne Page. Ten thousand honors and blessings on the bard who has thus gilded the dull realities of life with innocent illusions; who has spread exquisite and unbought pleasures in my checkered path; and beguiled my spirit in many a lonely hour, with all the cordial and cheerful sympathies of social life!

As I crossed the bridge over the Avon on my return, I paused to contemplate the distant church in which the poet lies buried, and could not but exult in the malediction, which has kept his ashes undisturbed in its quiet and hallowed vaults. What honor could his name have derived from being mingled in dusty companionship with the epitaphs and escutcheons and venal eulogiums of a titled multitude? What would a crowded corner in Westminster Abbey have been, compared with this reverend pile, which seems to stand in beautiful loneliness as his sole mausoleum! The solicitude about the grave may be but the offspring of an over-wrought sensibility; but human nature is made up of foibles and prejudices; and its best and tenderest affections are mingled with these factitious feelings. He who has sought renown about the world, and has reaped a full harvest of worldly favor, will find, after all, that there is no love, no admiration, no applause, so sweet to the soul as that which springs up in his native place. It is there that he seeks to be gathered in peace and honor among his kindred and his early friends. And when the weary heart and failing head begin to warn him that the evening of life is drawing on, he turns as fondly as does the infant to the mother's arms, to sink to sleep in the bosom of the scene of his childhood.

How would it have cheered the spirit of the youthful bard when, wandering forth in disgrace upon a doubtful world, he cast back a heavy look upon his paternal home, could he have foreseen that, before many years, he should return to it covered with renown; that his name should become the boast and glory of his native place; that his ashes should be religiously guarded as its most precious treasure; and that its lessening spire, on which his eyes were fixed in tearful contemplation, should one day become the beacon, towering amidst the gentle landscape, to guide the literary pilgrim of every nation to his tomb!

NOTES

[1] The following is the only stanza extant of this lampoon.—

> A parliament member, a justice of peace,
> At home a poor scarecrow, at London an asse,
> If lowsie is Lucy, as some volke miscalle it,
> Then Lucy is lowsie, whatever befall it.
>> He thinks himself great;
>> Yet an asse in his state,
> We allow by his ears but with asses to mate,
> If Lucy is lowsie, as some volke miscalle it,
> Then sing lowsie Lucy whatever befall it.

[2] The luce is a pike or jack, and abounds in the Avon about Charlecot.

[3] A proof of Shakspeare's random habits and associates in his youthful days may be found in a traditionary anecdote, picked up at Stratford by the elder Ireland, and mentioned in his "Picturesque Views on the Avon."

About seven miles from Stratford lies the thirsty little market-town of Bedford, famous for its ale. Two societies of the village yeomanry used to meet, under the appellation of the Bedford topers, and to challenge the lovers of good ale of the neighboring villages to a contest of drinking. Among others, the people of Stratford were called out to prove the strength of their heads; and in the number of the champions was Shakspeare, who, in spite of the proverb that "they who drink beer will think beer," was as true to his ale as Falstaff to his sack. The chivalry of Stratford was staggered at the first onset, and sounded a retreat while they had yet legs to carry them off the field. They had scarcely marched a mile when, their legs failing them, they were forced to lie down under a crab-tree, where they passed the night. It is still standing, and goes by the name of Shakspeare's tree.

In the morning his companions awaked the bard, and proposed returning to Bedford, but he declined, saying he had had enough, having drank with

> Piping Pebworth, Dancing Marston,
> Haunted Hilbro', Hungry Grafton,
> Dudging Exhall, Papist Wicksford,
> Beggarly Broom, and Drunken Bedford.

"The villages alluded to," says Ireland, "still bear the epithets thus given them: the people of Pebworth are still famed for their skill on the pipe and tabor; Hilborough is now called Haunted Hilborough; and Grafton is famous for the poverty of its soil."

[4]Scot, in his "Discoverie of Witchcraft," enumerates a host of these fireside fancies. "And they have so fraid us with bull-beggars, spirits, witches, urchins, elves, hags, fairies, satyrs, pan, faunes, syrens, kit with the can sticke, tritons, centaurs, dwarfes, gaintes, imps, calcars, conjurors, nymphes, changelings, incubus, Robin-good-fellow, the spoorne, the mare, the man in the oke, the hellwaine, the fier drake, the puckle, Tom Thombe, hobgoblins, Tom Tumbler, bootless, and such other bugs, that we were afraid of our own shadowes."

⁵This effigy is in white marble, and represents the Knight in complete armor. Near him lies the effigy of his wife, and on her tomb is the following inscription; which, if really composed by her husband, places him quite above the intellectual level of Master Shallow:

> "Here lyeth the Lady Joyce Lucy wife of Sir Thomas Lucy of Charlecot in ye county of Warwick, Knight, Daughter and heir of Thomas Acton of Sutton in ye county of Worcester Esquire who departed out of this wretched world to her heavenly kingdom ye 10 of February in ye yeare of our Lord God 1595 and of her age 60 and three. All the time of her lyfe a true and faythful servant of her good God, never detected of any cryme or vice. In religion most sounde, in love to her husband most faythful and true. In friendship most constant; to what in trust was committed unto her most secret. In wisdom excelling. In governing of her house, bringing up of youth in ye fear of God that did converse with her moste rare and singular. A great maintayner of hospitality. Greatly esteemed of her betters; misliked of none unless of the envyous. When all is spoken that can be saide a woman so garnished with virtue as not to be bettered and hardly to be equalled by any. As shee lived most virtuously so shee died most godly. Set downe by him yt best did knowe what hath byn written to be true.
>
> Thomas Lucye."

⁶Bishop Earle, speaking of the country gentleman of his time, observes, "his housekeeping is seen much in the different families of dogs, and serving-men attendant on their kennels; and the deepness of their throats is the depth of his discourse. A hawk he esteems the true burden of nobility, and is exceedingly ambitious to seem delighted with the sport, and have his fist gloved with his jesses." And Gilpin, in his description of a Mr. Hastings, remarks, "he kept all sorts of hounds that run buck, fox, hare, otter, and badger; and had hawks of all kinds both long and short

winged. His great hall was commonly strewed with marrowbones, and full of hawk-perches, hounds, spaniels, and terriers. On a broad hearth, paved with brick, lay some of the choicest terriers, hounds, and spaniels."

AN ARKANSAW DIFFICULTY

Mark Twain

It was after sun-up now, but we went right on and didn't tie up. The king and the duke turned out by and by looking pretty rusty; but after they'd jumped overboard and took a swim it chippered them up a good deal. After breakfast the king he took a seat on the corner of the raft, and pulled off his boots and rolled up his britches, and let his legs dangle in the water, so as to be comfortable, and lit his pipe, and went to getting his "Romeo and Juliet" by heart. When he had got it pretty good him and the duke begun to practise it together. The duke had to learn him over and over again how to say every speech; and he made him sigh, and put his hand on his heart, and after a while he said he done it pretty well; "only," he says, "you mustn't bellow out Romeo that way, like a bull—you must say it soft and sick and languishy, so—R-o-o-meo! that is the idea; for Juliet's a dear sweet mere child of a girl, you know, and she doesn't bray like a jackass."

Well, next they got out a couple of long swords that the duke made out of oak laths, and begun to practise the sword-fight—the duke called himself Richard III.; and the way they laid on and pranced around the raft was grand to see. But by and by the king tripped and fell overboard, and after that they took a rest, and had a talk about all kinds of adventures they'd had in other times along the river.

After dinner the duke says:

"Well, Capet, we'll want to make this a first-class show, you know, so I guess we'll add a little more to it. We want a little something to answer encores with, anyway."

"What's onkores, Bilgewater?"

The duke told him, and then says:

"I'll answer by doing the Highland fling or the sailor's hornpipe; and you—well, let me see—oh, I've got it—you can do Hamlet's soliloquy."

"Hamlet's which?"

"Hamlet's soliloquy, you know; the most celebrated thing in Shakespeare. Ah, it's sublime, sublime! Always fetches the house. I haven't got it in the book—I've only got one volume—but I reckon I can piece it out from memory. I'll just walk up and down a minute, and see if I can call it back from recollection's vaults."

So he went to marching up and down, thinking, and frowning horrible every now and then; then he would hoist up his eyebrows; next he would squeeze his hand on his forehead and stagger back and kind of moan; next he would sigh, and next he'd let on to drop a tear. It was beautiful to see him. By and by he got it. He told us to give attention. Then he strikes a most noble attitude, with one leg shoved forwards, and his arms stretched away up, and his head tilted back, looking up at the sky; and then he begins to rip and rave and grit his teeth; and after that, all through his speech, he howled, and spread around, and swelled up his chest, and just knocked the spots out of any acting ever *I* see before. This is the speech—I learned it, easy enough, while he was learning it to the king:

> *To be, or not to be; that is the bare bodkin*
> *That makes calamity of so long life;*
> *For who would fardels bear, till Birnam Wood do come to*
> *Dunsinane,*
> *But that the fear of something after death*
> *Murders the innocent sleep,*
> *Great nature's second course,*
> *And makes us rather sling the arrows of outrageous fortune*
> *Than fly to others that we know not of.*
> *There's the respect must give us pause:*
> *Wake Duncan with thy knocking! I would thou couldst;*
> *For who would bear the whips and scorns of time,*
> *The oppressor's wrong, the proud man's contumely,*
> *The law's delay, and the quietus which his pangs might take,*
> *In the dead waste and middle of the night, when churchyards*
> *yawn*
> *In customary suits of solemn black,*
> *But that the undiscovered country from whose bourne no traveler*
> *returns,*
> *Breathes forth contagion on the world,*
> *And thus the native hue of resolution, like the poor cat i' the*
> *adage,*
> *Is sicklied o'er with care,*
> *And all the clouds that lowered o'er our housetops,*
> *With this regard their currents turn awry,*
> *And lose the name of action.*
> *'Tis a consummation devoutly to be wished. But soft you, the*
> *fair Ophelia:*
> *Ope not thy ponderous and marble jaws,*
> *But get thee to a nunnery—go*

Well, the old man he liked that speech, and he mighty soon got it so he could do it first rate. It seemed like he was just born for it; and when he had his hand in and was excited, it was perfectly lovely the way he would rip and tear and rair up behind when he was getting it off.

The first chance we got the duke he had some show-bills printed; and after that, for two or three days as we floated along, the raft was a most uncommon lively place, for there warn't nothing but sword-fighting and rehearsing—as the duke called it—going on all the time. One morning, when we was pretty well down the state of Arkansaw, we come in sight of a little one-horse town in a big bend; so we tied up about three-quarters of a mile above it, in the mouth of a crick which was shut in like a tunnel by the cypress trees, and all of us but Jim took the canoe and went down there to see if there was any chance in that place for our show.

We struck it might lucky; there was going to be a circus there that afternoon, and the country-people was already beginning to come in, all kinds of old shackly wagons, and on horses. The circus would leave before night, so our show would have a pretty good chance. The duke he hired the court-house, and we went around and stuck up our bills. They read like this:

Shaksperean Revival
Wonderful Attraction
For One Night Only
The world renowned tragedians,
David Garrick the younger, of Drury Lane Theatre, London,
and
Edmund Kean the elder, of the Royal Haymarket Theatre,
Whitechapel, Pudding Lane, Piccadilly, London, and the
Royal Continental Theatres, in their sublime
Shaksperean Spectacle entitled
The Balcony Scene
in
Romeo and Juliet ! ! !

Romeo ....Mr. Garrick

Juliet ....Mr. Kean
Assisted by the whole strength of the company!
New costumes, new scenery, new appointments!
Also:
The thrilling, masterly, and blood-curdling
Broad-sword conflict
In Richard III. ! ! !
Richard III ....Mr. Garrick
Richmond ....Mr. Kean

Also:
(by special request)
Hamlet's Immortal Soliloquy ! !
By the Illustrious Kean
Done by him 300 consecutive nights in Paris!
For One Night Only,
On account of imperative European engagements!
Admission 25 cents; children and servants, 10 cents.

Then we went loafing around town. The stores and houses was most all old, shackly, dried-up frame concerns that hadn't ever been painted; they was set up three or four foot above ground on stilts, so as to be out of reach of the water when the river was overflowed. The houses had little gardens around them, but they didn't seem to raise hardly anything in them but jimpson-weeds, and sunflowers, and ash-piles, and old curled-up boots and shoes, and pieces of bottles, and rags, and played-out tinware. The fences was made of different kinds of boards, nailed on at different times; and they leaned every which way, and had gates that didn't generly have but one hinge—a leather one. Some of the fences had been whitewashed some time or another, but the duke said it was in Columbus's time, like enough. There was generly hogs in the garden, and people driving them out.

All the stores was along one street. They had white domestic awnings in front, and the country-people hitched their horses to the awning-posts. There was empty dry-goods boxes under the awnings, and loafers roosting on them all day long, whittling them with their Barlow knives; and chawing tobacco, and gaping and yawning and stretching—a might ornery lot. They generly had on yellow straw hats most as wide as an umbrella, but didn't wear no coats nor waistcoats; they called one another Bill, and Buck, and Hank, and Joe, and Andy, and talked lazy and drawly, and used considerable many cuss-words. There was as many as one loafer leaning up against every awning-post, and he most always had his hands in his britches pockets, except when he fetched them out to lend a chaw of tobacco or scratch. What a body was hearing amongst them all the time was:

"Gimme a chaw 'v tobacker, Hank."

"Cain't; I hain't got but one chaw left. Ask Bill."

Maybe Bill he gives him a chaw; maybe he lies and says he ain't got none. Some of them kinds of loafers never has a cent in the world, nor a chaw of tobacco of their own. They get all their chawing by borrowing; they say to a fellow, "I wisht you'd len' me a chaw, Jack, I jist this minute give Ben Thompson the last chaw I had"—which is a lie pretty much every time; it don't fool nobody but a stranger; but Jack ain't no stranger, so he says:

"*You* give him a chaw, did you? So did your sister's cat's grandmother. You pay me back the chaws you've awready borry'd off'n me, Lafe Buckner, then I'll loan you one or two ton of it, and won't charge you no back intrust, nuther."

"Well, I *did* pay you back some of it wunst."

"Yes, you did—'bout six chaws. You borry'd store tobacker and paid back nigger-head."

Store tobacco is flat black plug, but these fellows mostly chaws the natural leaf twisted. When they borrow a chaw they don't generly cut it off with a knife, but set the plug in between their teeth, and gnaw with their teeth and tug at the plug with their hands till they get it in two; then sometimes the one that owns the tobacco looks mournful at it when it's handed back, and says, sarcastic:

"Here, gimme the *chaw*, and you take the *plug*."

All the streets and lanes was just mud; they warn't nothing else *but* mud—mud as black as tar and nigh about a foot deep in some places, and two or three inches deep in *all* the places. The hogs loafed and grunted around everywheres. You'd see a muddy sow and a litter of pigs come lazying along the street and whollop herself right down in the way, where folks had to walk around her, and she'd stretch out and shut her eyes and wave her ears whilst the pigs was milking her, and look as happy as if she was on salary. And pretty soon you'd hear a loafer sing out, "Hi! *so* boy! sick him, Tige!" and away the sow would go, squealing most horrible, with a dog or two swinging to each ear, and three or four dozen more a-coming; and then you would see all the loafers get up and watch the thing out of sight, and laugh at the fun and look grateful for the noise. Then they'd settle back again till there was a dog-fight. There couldn't anything wake them up all over, and make them happy all over, like a dog-fight—unless it might be putting turpentine on a stray dog and setting fire to him, or tying a tin pan to his tail and see him run himself to death.

On the river-front some of the houses was sticking out over the bank, and they was bowed and bent, and about ready to tumble in. The people had moved out of them. The bank was caved away under one corner of some others, and that corner was hanging over. People lived in them yet, but it was dangersome, because sometimes a strip of land as wide as a house caves in at a time. Sometimes a belt of land a quarter of a mile deep will start in and cave along and cave along till it all caves into the river in one summer. Such a town as that has to be always moving back, and back, and back, because the river's always gnawing at it.

The nearer it got to noon that day the thicker and thicker was the wagons and horses in the streets, and more coming all the time. Families fetched their dinners with them from the country, and eat them in the wagons. There was considerable whisky-drinking going on, and I seen three fights. By and by somebody sings out:

"Here comes old Boggs!—in from the country for his little old monthly drunk; here he comes, boys!"

All the loafers looked glad; I reckoned they was used to having fun out of Boggs. One of them says:

"Wonder who he's a-gwyne to chaw up this time. If he'd a-chawed up all the men he's ben a-gwyne to chaw up in the last twenty year he'd have considerable reputation now."

Another one says, "I wisht old Boggs 'd threaten me, 'cuz then I'd know I warn't gwyne to die for a thousan' year."

Boggs comes a-tearing along on his horse, whooping and yelling like an Injun, and singing out:

"Cler the track, thar. I'm on the waw-path, and the price uv coffins is a-gwyne to raise."

He was drunk, and weaving about in his saddle; he was over fifty year old, and had a very red face. Everybody yelled at him and laughed at him and sassed him, and he sassed back, and said he'd attend to them and lay them out in their regular turns, but he couldn't wait now because he'd come to town to kill old Colonel Sherburn, and his motto was, "Meat first and spoon vittles to top off on."

He see me, and rode up and says:

"Whar'd you come f'm, boy? You prepared to die?"

Then he rode on. I was scared, but a man says:

"He don't mean nothing; he's always a-carryin' on like that when he's drunk. He's the best-naturedest old fool in Arkansaw—never hurt nobody, drunk nor sober."

Boggs rode up before the biggest store in town, and bent his head down so he could see under the curtain of the awning and yells:

"Come out here, Sherburn! Come out and meet the man you've swindled. You're the houn' I'm after, and I'm a-gwyne to have you, too!"

And so he went on, calling Sherburn everything he could lay his tongue to, and the whole street packed with people listening and laughing and going on. By and by a proud-looking man about fifty-five—and he was a heap the best-dressed man in that town, too—steps out of the store, and the crowd drops back on each side to let him come. He says to Boggs, mighty ca'm and slow—he says:

"I'm tired of this, but I'll endure it till one o'clock. Till one o'clock, mind—no longer. If you open your mouth against me only once after that time you can't travel so far but I will find you."

Then he turns and goes in. The crowed looked mighty sober; nobody stirred, and there warn't no more laughing. Boggs rode off blackguarding Sherburn as loud as he could yell, all down the street; and pretty soon back he comes and stops before the store, still keeping it up. Some men crowded around him and tried to get him to shut up, but he wouldn't; they told him it would be one o'clock in about fifteen minutes, and so he *must* go home—he must go right away. But it didn't do no good. He cussed away with all his might, and throwed his hat down in the mud and rode over it, and pretty soon away he went a-raging down the street again, with his gray hair a-flying. Everybody that could get a chance at him tried their best to coax him off of his horse so they could lock him up and get him sober; but it warn't no use—up the street he would tear again, and give Sherburn another cussing. By and by somebody says:

"Go for his daughter!—quick, go for his daughter; sometimes he'll listen to her. If anybody can persuade him, she can."

So somebody started on a run. I walked down street a ways and stopped. In about five or ten minutes here comes Boggs again, but not on his horse. He was a-reeling across the street towards me, bareheaded, with a friend on both sides of him a-holt of his arms and hurrying him along. He was quiet, and looked uneasy; and he warn't hanging back any, but was doing some of the hurrying himself. Somebody sings out:

"Boggs!"

I looked over there to see who said it, and it was that Colonel Sherburn. He was standing perfectly still in the street, and had a pistol raised in his right hand—not aiming it, but holding it out with the barrel tilted up towards the sky. The same second I see a young girl coming on the run, and two men with her. Boggs and the men turned round to see who called him, and when they see the pistol the men jumped to one side, and the pistol-barrel come down slow and steady to a level—both barrels cocked. Boggs throws up both of his hands and says, "O Lord, don't shoot!" Bang! goes the first shot, and he staggers back, clawing at the air— bang! goes the second one, and he tumbles backwards onto the ground, heavy and solid, with his arms spread out. That young girl screamed out and comes rushing, and down she throws herself on her father, crying, and saying, "Oh, he's killed him, he's killed him!" The crowd closed up around them, and shouldered and jammed one another, with their necks stretched, trying to see, and people on the inside trying to shove them back and shouting,

"Back, back! give him air, give him air!"

Colonel Sherburn he tossed his pistol onto the ground, and turned around on his heels and walked off.

They took Boggs to a little drug store, the crowd pressing around just the same, and the whole town following, and I rushed and got a good place at the window, where I was close to him and could see in. They laid him on the floor and put one large Bible under his head, and opened another one and spread it on his breast; but they tore open his shirt first, and I seen where one of the bullets went in. He made about a dozen long gasps, his breast lifting the Bible up when he drawed in his breath, and letting it down again when he breathed it out—and after that he laid still; he was dead. Then they pulled his daughter away from him, screaming and crying, and took her off. She was about sixteen, and very sweet and gentle looking, but awful pale and scared.

Well, pretty soon the whole town was there, squirming and scrouging and pushing and shoving to get at the window and have a look, but people that had the places wouldn't give them up, and folks behind them was saying all the time, "Say, now, you've looked enough, you fellows; 'tain't right and 'tain't fair for you to stay thar all the time, and never give nobody a chance; other folks has their rights as well as you."

There was considerable jawing back, so I slid out, thinking maybe there was going to be trouble. The streets was full, and everybody was excited. Everybody that seen the shooting was telling how it happened, and there was a big crowd packed around each one of these fellows, stretching their necks and listening. One long, lanky man, with long hair and a big white fur stovepipe hat on the back of his head, and a crooked-handled cane, marked out the places on the ground where Boggs stood and where Sherburn stood, and the people following him around from one place to t'other and watching everything he done, and bobbing their heads to show they understood, and stooping a little and resting their hands on their thighs to watch him mark the places on the ground with his cane; and then he stood up straight and stiff where Sherburn had stood, frowning and having his hat-brim down over his eyes, and sung out, "Boggs!" and then fetched his cane down slow to a level, and says "Bang!" staggered backwards, says "Bang!" again, and fell down flat on his back. The people that had seen the thing said he done it perfect; said it was just exactly the way it all happened. Then as much as a dozen people got out their bottles and treated him.

Well, by and by somebody said Sherburn ought to be lynched. In about a minute everybody was saying it; so away they went, mad and yelling, and snatching down every clothes-line they come to to do the hanging with.

From *GREAT EXPECTATIONS*

Charles Dickens

On our arrival in Denmark, we found the king and queen of that country elevated in two arm-chairs on a kitchen-table, holding a Court. The whole of the Danish nobility were in attendance; consisting of a noble boy in the wash-leather boots of a gigantic ancestor, a venerable Peer with a dirty face, who seemed to have risen from the people late in life, and the Danish chivalry with a comb in its hair and a pair of white silk legs, and presenting on the whole a feminine appearance. My gifted townsman stood gloomily apart, with folded arms, and I could have wished that his curls and forehead had been more probable.

Several curious little circumstances transpired as the action proceeded. The late king of the country not only appeared to have been troubled with a cough at the time of his decease, but to have taken it with him to the tomb, and to have brought it back. The royal phantom also carried a ghostly manuscript round its truncheon, to which it had the appearance of occasionally referring, and that, too, with an air of anxiety and a tendency to lose the place of reference which were suggestive of a state of mortality. It was this, I conceive, which led to the Shake's being advised by the gallery to "turn over!"—a recommendation which it took extremely ill. It was likewise to be noted of this majestic spirit that whereas it always appeared with an air of having been out a long time and walked an immense distance, it perceptibly came from a closely-contiguous wall. This occasioned its terrors to be received derisively. The Queen of Denmark, a very buxom lady, though no doubt historically brazen, was considered by the public to have too much brass about her; her chin being attached to her diadem by a broad band of that metal (as if she had a gorgeous toothache), her waist being encircled by another, and each of her arms by another, so that she was openly mentioned as "the kettle-drum." The noble boy in the ancestral boots, was inconsistent; representing himself, as it were in one breath, as an able seaman, a strolling actor, a grave-digger, a clergyman, and a person of the utmost importance at a Court fencing-match, on the authority of whose practised eye and nice discrimination the finest strokes were judged. This gradually led to a want of toleration for him, and even—on his being detected in holy orders, and declining to perform the funeral service—to the general indignation taking the form of nuts. Lastly, Ophelia was a prey to such slow musical madness, that when, in course of time, she had taken off her white muslin scarf, folded it up, and buried it, a sulky man who had been long cooling his impatient nose against an iron bar in the front row of the gallery, growled, "Now the baby's put to bed, let's have supper!" Which, to say the least of it, was out of keeping.

Upon my unfortunate townsman all these incidents accumulated with playful effect. Whenever that undecided

Prince had to ask a question or state a doubt, the public helped him out with it. As for example; on the question whether 'twas nobler in the mind to suffer, some roared yes, and some no, and some inclining to both opinions said "toss up for it"; and quite a Debating Society arose. When he asked what should such fellows as he do crawling between earth and heaven, he was encouraged with loud cries of "Hear, hear!" When he appeared with his stocking disordered (its disorder expressed, according to usage, by one very neat fold in the top, which I suppose to be always got up with a flat iron), a conversation took place in the gallery respecting the paleness of his leg, and whether it was occasioned by the turn the ghost had given him. On his taking the recorders—very like a little black flute that had just been played in the orchestra and handed out at the door—he was called upon unanimously for Rule Britannia. When he recommended the player not to saw the air thus, the sulky man said, "And don't *you* do it, neither; you're a deal worse than *him*!" And I grieve to add that peals of laughter greeted Mr. Wopsle on every one of these occasions.

But his greatest trials were in the churchyard: which had the appearance of a primeval forest, with a kind of small ecclesiastical wash-house on one side, and a turnpike gate on the other. Mr. Wopsle, in a comprehensive black cloak, being descried entering at the turnpike, the grave-digger was admonished in a friendly way, "Look out! Here's the undertaker a-coming, to see how you're getting on with your work!" I believe it is well known in a constitutional country that Mr. Wopsle could not possibly have returned the skull, after moralizing over it, without dusting his fingers on a white napkin taken from his breast; but even that innocent and indispensable action did not pass without the comment "Wai-ter!" The arrival of the body for interment (in an empty black box with the lid tumbling open), was the signal for a general joy which was much enhanced by the discovery, among the bearers, of an individual obnoxious to identification. The joy attended Mr. Wopsle through his struggle with Laertes on the brink of the orchestra and the grave, and slackened no more until he had tumbled the king off the kitchen-table, and had died by inches from the ankles upwards.

We had made some pale efforts in the beginning to applaud Mr. Wopsle; but they were too hopeless to be persisted in. Therefore we had sat, feeling keenly for him, but laughing, nevertheless, from ear to ear. I laughed in spite of myself all the time, the whole thing was so droll; and yet I had a latent impression that there was something decidedly fine in Mr. Wopsle's elocution—not for old associations' sake, I am afraid, but because it was very slow, very dreary, very up-hill and down-hill, and very unlike any way in which any man in any natural circumstances of life or death ever expressed himself about anything. When the tragedy was over, and he had been called for and hooted, I said to Herbert, "Let us go at once, or perhaps we shall meet him."

We made all the haste we could downstairs, but we were not quick enough either. Standing at the door was a Jewish man with an unnatural heavy smear of eyebrow, who caught my eyes as we advanced, and said, when we came up with him:

"Mr. Pip and friend?"

Identity of Mr. Pip and friend confessed.

"Mr. Waldengarver," said the man, "would be glad to have the honour."

"Waldengarver," I repeated—when Herbert murmured in my ear, "Probably Wopsle."

"Oh!" said I. "Yes. Shall we follow you?"

"A few steps, please." When we were in a side alley, he turned and asked, "How do you think he looked?—*I* dressed him."

I don't know what he had looked like, except a funeral; with the addition of a large Danish sun or star hanging round his neck by a blue ribbon, that had given him the appearance of being insured in some extraordinary Fire Office. But I said he had looked very nice.

"When he come to the grave," said our conductor, "he showed his cloak beautiful. But, judging from the wing, it looked to me that when he see the ghost in the queen's apartment, he might have made more of his stockings."

I modestly assented, and we all fell through a little dirty swing door, into a sort of hot packing-case immediately behind it. Here Mr. Wopsle was divesting himself of his Danish garments, and here there was just room for us to look at him over one another's shoulders, by keeping the packing-case door, or lid, wide open.

"Gentleman," said Mr. Wopsle, "I am proud to see you. I hope, Mr. Pip, you will excuse my sending round. I had the happiness to know you in former times, and the Drama has ever had a claim which has ever been acknowledged, on the noble and the affluent."

Meanwhile, Mr. Waldengarver, in a frightful perspiration, was trying to get himself out of his princely sables.

"Skin the stockings off, Mr. Waldengarver," said the owner of that property, "or you'll bust 'em. Bust 'em, and you'll bust five-and-thirty shillings. Shakespeare never was complimented with a finer pair. Keep quiet in your chair now, and leave 'em to me."

With that, he went upon his knees, and began to flay his victim; who, on the first stocking coming off, would certainly have fallen over backward with his chair, but for there being no room to fall anyhow.

I had been afraid until then to say a word about the play. But then, Mr. Waldengarver looked up at us complacently, and said:

"Gentlemen, how did it seem to you, to go, in front?"

Herbert said from behind (at the same time poking me), "capitally." So I said "capitally."

"How did you like my reading of the character, gentlemen?" said Mr. Waldengarver, almost, if not quite, with patronage.

Herbert said from behind (again poking me), "massive and concrete." So I said boldly, as if I had originated it, and must bet to insist upon, it, "massive and concrete."

"I am glad to have your approbation, gentlemen," said Mr. Waldengarver, with an air of dignity, in spite of his being ground against the wall at the time, and holding on by the seat of the chair.

"But I'll tell you one thing, Mr. Waldengarver," said the man who was on his knees, "in which you're out in your reading. Now mind! I don't care who says contrary; I tell you so. You're out in your reading of Hamlet when you get your legs in profile. The last Hamlet as I dressed, made the same mistakes in his reading at rehearsal, till I got him to put a large red wafer on each of his shins, and then at that rehearsal (which was the last) I went in front, sir, to the back of the pit, and whenever his reading brought him into profile, I called out, 'I don't see no wafer!' And at night his reading was lovely."

Mr. Waldengarver smiled at me, as much as to say "a faithful dependent—I overlook his folly"; and then said aloud, "My view is a little classic and thoughtful for them here; but they will improve, they will improve."

Herbert and I said together, Oh, no doubt they would improve.

"Did you observe, gentlemen," said Mr. Waldengarver, "that there was a man in the gallery who endeavoured to cast derision on the service—I mean, the representation?"

We basely replied that we rather thought we had noticed such a man. I added, "He was drunk, no doubt."

"Oh dear no, sir," said Mr. Wopsle, "not drunk. His employer would see to that, sir. His employer would not allow him to be drunk."

"You know his employer?" said I.

Mr. Wopsle shut his eyes, and opened them again; performing both ceremonies very slowly. "You must have observed, gentlemen," said he, "an ignorant and a blatant ass, with a rasping throat and a countenance expressive of low malignity, who went through—I will not say sustained—the rôle (if I may use a French expression) of Claudius King of Denmark. That is his employer, gentleman. Such is the profession!"

Without distinctly knowing whether I should have been more sorry for Mr. Wopsle if he had been in despair, I was so sorry for him as it was, that I took the opportunity of his turning round to have his braces put on—which jostled us out at the doorway—to ask Herbert what he thought of having him home to supper? Herbert said he thought it would be kind to do so; therefore I invited him, and he went to Barnard's with us, wrapped up to the eyes, and we did our best for him, and he sat until two o'clock in the morning, reviewing his success and developing his plans. I forget in detail what they were, but I have a general recollection that he was to begin with reviving the Drama, and to end with crushing it; inasmuch as his decease would leave it utterly bereft and without a chance or hope.

Miserably I went to bed after all, and miserably thought of Estella, and miserably dreamed that my expectations were all cancelled, and that I had to give my hand in marriage to Herbert's Clara, or play Hamlet to Miss Havisham's Ghost, before twenty thousand people, without knowing twenty words of it.

THE PORTRAIT OF MR W. H.

Oscar Wilde

I had been dining with Erskine in his pretty little house in Birdcage Walk, and we were sitting in the library over our coffee and cigarettes, when the question of literary forgeries happened to turn up in conversation. I cannot at present remember how it was that we struck upon this somewhat curious topic, as it was at that time, but I know that we had a long discussion about Macpherson, Ireland, and Chatterton, and that with regard to the last I insisted that his so-called forgeries were merely the result of an artistic desire for perfect representation: that we had no right to quarrel with an artist for the conditions under which he chooses to present his work; and that all Art being to a certain degree a mode of acting, an attempt to realise one's own personality on some imaginative plane out of reach of the trammeling accidents and limitations of real life, to censure an artist for a forgery was to confuse an ethical with an aesthetical problem.

Erskine, who was a good deal older than I was, and had been listening to me with the amused deference of a man of forty, suddenly put his hand upon my shoulder and said to me, "What would you say about a young man who had a strange theory about a certain work of art, believed in his theory, and committed a forgery in order to prove it?"

"Ah! that is quite a different matter," I answered.

Erskine remained silent for a few moments, looking at the thin grey threads of smoke that were rising from his cigarette. "Yes," he said, after a pause, "quite different."

There was something in the tone of his voice, a slight touch of bitterness perhaps, that excited my curiosity. "Did you ever know anybody who did that?" I cried.

"Yes," he answered, throwing his cigarette into the fire,—"a great friend of mine, Cyril Graham. He was very fascinating, and very foolish, and very heartless. However, he left me the only legacy I ever received in my life."

"What was that?" I exclaimed. Erskine rose from his seat, and going over to a tall inlaid cabinet that stood between the two windows, unlocked it, and came back to where I was sitting, holding in his hand a small panel picture set in an old and somewhat tarnished Elizabethan frame.

It was a full-length portrait of a young man in the late sixteenth-century costume, standing by a table, with his right hand resting on an open book. He seemed about seventeen years of age, and was of quite extraordinary personal beauty, though evidently somewhat effeminate. Indeed, had it not been for the dress and the closely cropped hair, one would have said that the face, with its dreamy wistful eyes, and its delicate scarlet lips, was the face of a girl. In manner, and especially in the treatment of the hands, the picture reminded one of François Clouet's later work. The black velvet doublet with its fantastically gilded points, and the peacock-blue background against which it showed up so pleasantly, and from which it gained such luminous value of colour, were quite in Clouet's style; and the two masks of Tragedy and Comedy that hung somewhat formally from the marble pedestal had that hard severity of touch—no different from the facile grace of the Italians—which even at the Court of France the great Flemish master never completely lost, and which in itself has always been a characteristic of the northern temper.

"It is a charming thing," I cried; "but who is this wonderful young man, whose beauty Art has so happily preserved for us?"

"This is the portrait of Mr W. H.," said Erskine, with a sad smile. It might have been a chance effect of light, but it seemed to me that his eyes were quite bright with tears.

"Mr W. H.!" I exclaimed; "who was Mr W. H.?"

"Don't you remember?" he answered; "look at the book on which his hand is resting."

"I see there is some writing there, but I cannot make it out," I replied.

"Take this magnifying glass and try," said Erskine, with the same sad smile still playing about his mouth.

I took the glass, and moving the lamp a little nearer, I began to spell out the crabbed sixteenth-century handwriting. "To the onlie begetter of these insuing sonnets." . . . "Good heavens!" I cried, "is this Shakespeare's Mr W. H.?"

"Cyril Graham used to say so," muttered Erskine.

"But it is not a bit like Lord Pembroke," I answered. "I know the Penshurst portraits very well. I was staying near there a few weeks ago."

"Do you really believe then that the Sonnets are addressed to Lord Pembroke?" he asked.

"I am sure of it," I answered. "Pembroke, Shakespeare, and Mrs Mary Fitton are the three personages of the Sonnets; there is no doubt at all about it."

"Well, I agree with you," said Erskine, "but I did not always think so. I used to believe—well, I suppose I used to believe in Cyril Graham and his theory."

"And what was that?" I asked, looking at the wonderful portrait, which had already begun to have a strange fascination for me.

"It is a long story," said Erskine, taking the picture away from me—rather abruptly I thought at the time—"a very long story; but if you care to hear it, I will tell it to you."

"I love theories about the Sonnets," I cried; "but I don't think I am likely to be converted to any new idea. The matter has ceased to be a mystery to any one. Indeed, I wonder that it ever was a mystery."

"As I don't believe in the theory, I am not likely to convert you to it," said Erskine, laughing; "but it may interest you."

"Tell it to me, of course," I answered. "If it is half as delightful as the picture I shall be more than satisfied."

"Well," said Erskine, lighting a cigarette, "I must begin by telling you about Cyril Graham himself. He and I were at the same house at Eton. I was a year or two older than he was, but we were immense friends, and did all our work and all our play together. There was, of course, a good deal more play than work, but I cannot say that I am sorry for that. It is always an advantage not to have received a sound commercial education, and what I learned in the playing fields at Eton has been quite as useful to me as anything I was taught at Cambridge. I should tell you that Cyril's father and mother were both dead. They had been drowned in a horrible yachting accident off the Isle of Wight. His father had been in the diplomatic service, and had married a daughter, the only daughter, in fact, of old Lord Crediton, who became Cyril's guardian after the death of his parents. I don't think that Lord Crediton cared very much for Cyril. He had never really forgiven his daughter for marrying a man who had no title. He was an extraordinary old aristocrat, who swore like a costermonger, and had the manners of a farmer. I remember seeing him once on Speech-day. He growled at me, gave me a sovereign, and told me not to grow up 'a damned Radical' like my father. Cyril had very little affection for him, and was only too glad to spend most of his holidays with us in Scotland. They never really got on together at all. Cyril thought him a bear, and he thought Cyril effeminate. He was effeminate, I suppose, in some things, though he was a very good rider and a capital fencer. In fact he got the foils before he left Eton. But he was very languid in his manner, and not a little vain of his good looks, and had a strong objection to football. The two things that really gave him pleasure were poetry and acting. At Eton he was always dressing up and reciting Shakespeare, and when we went up to Trinity he became a member of the A.D.C. his first term. I remember I was always very jealous of his acting. I was absurdly devoted to him; I suppose because we were so different in some things. I was a rather awkward, weakly lad, with huge feet, and horribly freckled. Freckles run in Scotch families just as gout does in English families. Cyril used to say that of the two he preferred the gout; but he always set an absurdly high value on personal appearance, and once read a paper before our debating society to prove that it was better to be good-looking than to be good. He certainly was wonderfully handsome. People who did not like him, Philistines and college tutors, and young men reading for the Church, used to say that he was merely pretty; but there was a great deal more in his face than mere prettiness. I think he was the most splendid creature I ever saw, and nothing could exceed the grace of his movements, the charm of his manner. He fascinated everybody who was worth fascinating, and a great many people who were not.

He was often wilful and petulant, and I used to think him dreadfully insincere. It was due, I think, chiefly to his inordinate desire to please. Poor Cyril! I told him once that he was contented with very cheap triumphs, but he only laughed. He was horribly spoiled. All charming people, I fancy, are spoiled. It is the secret of their attraction.

"However, I must tell you about Cyril's acting. You know that no actresses are allowed to play at the A.D.C. At least they were not in my time. I don't know how it is now. Well, of course Cyril was always cast for the girls' parts, and when 'As You Like It' was produced he played Rosalind. It was a marvellous performance. In fact, Cyril Graham was the only perfect Rosalind I have ever seen. It would be impossible to describe to you the beauty, the delicacy, the refinement of the whole thing. It made an immense sensation, and the horrid little theatre, as it was then, was crowded every night. Even when I read the play now I can't help thinking of Cyril. It might have been written for him. The next term he took his degree, and came to London to read for the diplomatic. But he never did any work. He spent his days in reading Shakespeare's Sonnets, and his evenings at the theatre. He was, of course, wild to go on the stage. It was all that I and Lord Crediton could do to prevent him. Perhaps if he had gone on the stage he would be alive now. It is always a silly thing to give advice, but to give good advice is absolutely fatal. I hope you will never fall into that error. If you do, you will be sorry for it.

"Well, to come to the real point of the story, one day I got a letter from Cyril asking me to come round to his rooms that evening. He had charming chambers in Piccadilly overlooking the Green Park, and as I used to go to see him every day, I was rather surprised at his taking the trouble to write. Of course I went, and when I arrived I found him in a state of great excitement. He told me that he had at last discovered the true secret of Shakespeare's Sonnets; that all the scholars and critics had been entirely on the wrong tack; and that he was the first who, working purely by internal evidence, had found out who Mr W. H. really was. He was perfectly wild with delight, and for a long time would not tell me his theory. Finally, he produced a bundle of notes, took his copy of the Sonnets off the mantelpiece, and sat down and gave me a long lecture on the whole subject.

"He began by pointing out that the young man to whom Shakespeare addressed these strangely passionate poems must have been somebody who was a really vital factor in the development of his dramatic art, and that this could not be said either of Lord Pembroke or Lord Southampton. Indeed, whoever he was, he could not have been anybody of high birth, as was shown very clearly by the 25th Sonnet, in which Shakespeare contrasts himself with those who are 'great princes' favourites;' says quite frankly—

> "'Let those who are in favour with their stars
> Of public honour and proud titles boast,
> Whilst I, whom fortune of such triumph bars,
> Unlooked for joy in that I honour most;'

and ends the sonnet by congratulating himself on the mean state of him he so adored:

> "'Then happy I, that loved and am beloved
> Where I may not remove nor be removed.'

This sonnet Cyril declared would be quite unintelligible if we fancied that it was addressed to either the Earl of Pembroke or the Earl of Southampton, both of whom were men of the highest position in England and fully entitled to be called 'great princes'; and he in corroboration of his view read me

Sonnets cxxiv. and cxxv., in which Shakespeare tells us that his love is not 'the child of state,' that it 'suffers not in smiling pomp,' but is 'builded far from accident.' I listened with a good deal of interest, for I don't think the point had ever been made before; but what followed was still more curious, and seemed to me at the time to entirely dispose of Pembroke's claim. We know from Meres that the Sonnets had been written before 1598, and Sonnet civ. informs us that Shakespeare's friendship for Mr W. H. had been already in existence for three years. Now Lord Pembroke, who was born in 1580, and not come to London till he was eighteen years of age, that is to say till 1598, and Shakespeare's acquaintance with Mr W. H. must have begun in 1594, or at the latest in 1595. Shakespeare, accordingly, could not have known Lord Pembroke till after the Sonnets had been written.

   "Cyril pointed out also that Pembroke's father did not die till 1601; whereas it was evident from the line,

'You had a father, let your son say so,'

that the father of Mr W. H. was dead in 1598. Besides, it was absurd to imagine that any publisher of the time, and the preface is from the publisher's hand, would have ventured to address William Herbert, Earl of Pembroke, as Mr W. H.; the case of Lord Buckhurst being spoken of as Mr Sackville being not really a parallel instance, as Lord Buckhurst was not a peer, but merely the younger son of peer, with a courtesy title, and the passage in 'England's Parnassus,' where he is so spoken of, is not a formal and stately dedication, but simply a casual allusion. So far for Lord Pembroke, whose supposed claims Cyril easily demolished while I sat by in wonder. With Lord Southampton Cyril had even less difficulty. Southampton became at a very early age the lover of Elizabeth Vernon, so he needed no entreaties to marry; he was not beautiful; he did not resemble his mother, as Mr W. H. did—

"'Thou art thy mother's glass, and she in thee
Calls back the lovely April of her prime;'

and, above all, his Christian name was Henry, whereas the punning sonnets (cxxx. and cxlii.) show that the Christian name of Shakespeare's friend was the same as his own—*Will*.

"As for the other suggestions of unfortunate commentators, that Mr W. H. is a misprint for Mr W. S., meaning Mr William Shakespeare; that 'Mr W. H. all' should be read 'Mr W. Hall'; that Mr W. H. is Mr William Hathaway; and that a full stop should be placed after 'wisheth,' making Mr W. H. the writer and not the subject of the dedication,—Cyril got rid of them in a very short time; and it is not worth while to mention his reasons, though I remember he sent me off into a fit of laughter by reading to me, I am glad to say not in the original, some extracts from a German commentator called Barnstorff, who insisted that Mr W. H. was no less a person than 'Mr William Himself.' Nor would he allow for a moment that the Sonnets are mere satires on the work of Drayton and John Davies of Hereford. To him, as indeed to me, they were poems of serious and tragic import, wrung out of the bitterness of Shakespeare's heart, and made sweet by the honey of his lips. Still less would he admit that they were merely a philosophical allegory, and that in them Shakespeare is addressing his Ideal Self, or Ideal Manhood, or the Spirit of Beauty, or the Reason, or the Divine Logos, or the Catholic Church. He felt, as indeed I think we all must feel, that the Sonnets are addressed to an individual,—to a particular young man whose personality for some reason seems to have filled the soul of Shakespeare with terrible joy and no less terrible despair.

"Having in this manner cleared the way as it were, Cyril asked me to dismiss from my mind any preconceived ideas I might have formed on the subject, and to give a fair and unbiassed hearing to his own theory. The problem he pointed out was this: Who was that young man of Shakespeare's day who, without being of noble birth or even of noble nature, was addressed by him in terms of such passionate adoration that we can but wonder at the strange worship, and are almost afraid to turn the key that unlocks the mystery of the poet's heart? Who was he whose physical beauty was such that it became the very cornerstone of Shakespeare's art; the very source of Shakespeare's inspiration; the very incarnation of Shakespeare's dreams? To look upon him as simply the object of certain love-poems is to miss the whole meaning of the poems: for the art of which Shakespeare talks in the Sonnets is not the art of the Sonnets themselves, which indeed were to him but slight and secret things—it is the art of the dramatist to which he is always alluding; and he to whom Shakespeare said—

"'Thou art all my art, and dost advance
As high as learning my rude ignorance,'—

he to whom he promised immortality,

"'Where breath most breathes, even in the mouth of men,'—

was surely none other than the boy-actor for whom he created Viola and Imogen, Juliet and Rosalind, Portia and Desdemona, and Cleopatra herself. This was Cyril Graham's theory, evolved as you see purely from the

Sonnets themselves, and depending for its acceptance not so much on demonstrable proof or formal evidence, but on a kind of spiritual and artistic sense, by which alone he claimed could the true meaning of the poems be discerned. I remember his reading to me that fine sonnet—

> "'How can my Muse want subject to invent,
> While thou dost breathe, that pour'st into my verse
> Thine own sweet argument, too excellent
> For every vulgar paper to rehearse?
> O, give thyself the thanks, if aught in me
> Worthy perusal stand against thy sight;
> For who's so dumb that cannot write to thee,
> When thou thyself dost give invention light?
> Be thou the tenth Muse, ten times more in worth
> Than those old nine which rhymers invocate;
> And he that calls on thee, let him bring forth
> Eternal numbers to outlive long date'

—and pointing out how completely it corroborated his theory; and indeed he went through all the Sonnets carefully, and showed, or fancied that he showed, that, according to his new explanation of their meaning, things that had seemed obscure, or evil, or exaggerated, became clear and rational, and of high artistic import, illustrating Shakespeare's conception of the true relations between the art of the actor and the art of the dramatist.

"It is of course evident that there must have been in Shakespeare's company some wonderful boy-actor of great beauty, to whom he intrusted the presentation of his noble heroines; for Shakespeare was a practical theatrical manager as well as an imaginative poet, and Cyril Graham had actually discovered the boy-actor's name. He was Will, or, as he preferred to call him, Willie Hughes. The Christian name he found of course in the punning sonnets, cxxxv. and

cxliii.; the surname was, according to him, hidden in the
eighth line of the 20th Sonnet, where Mr W. H. is described
as—

> "'A man in hew, all *Hews* in his controwling.'

"In the original edition of the Sonnets "Hews" is printed
with a capital letter and in italics, and this, he claimed,
showed clearly that a play on words was intended, his view
receiving a good deal of corroboration from those sonnets in
which curious puns are made on the words 'use' and
'usury.' Of course I was converted at once, and Willie
Hughes became to me as real a person as Shakespeare. The
only objection I made to the theory was that the name of
Willie Hughes does not occur in the list of the actors of
Shakespeare's company as it is printed in the first folio.
Cyril, however, pointed out that the absence of Willie
Hughes's name from this list really corroborated the theory,
as it was evident from Sonnet lxxxvi. that Willie Hughes had
abandoned Shakespeare's company to play at a rival theatre,
probably in some of Chapman's plays. It is in reference to
this that in the great sonnet on Chapman Shakespeare said to
Willie Hughes—

> "'But when your countenance filled up his line,
> Then lacked I matter; that enfeebled mine'—

the expression 'when your countenance filled up his line'
referring obviously to the beauty of the young actor giving
life and reality and added charm to Chapman's verse, the
same idea being also put forward in the 79th Sonnet—

> "'Whilst I alone did call upon thy aid,
> My verse alone had all thy gentle grace.

> But now my gracious numbers are decayed,
> And my sick Muse does give another place;'

and in the immediately preceding sonnet, where Shakespeare says,

> '"Every alien pen has got my *use*
> And under thee their poesy disperse.'

the play upon words (use = Hughes) being of course obvious, and the phrase 'under thee their poesy disperse,' meaning 'by your assistance as an actor bring their plays before the people.'

"It was a wonderful evening, and we sat up almost till dawn reading and re-reading the Sonnets. After some time, however, I began to see that before the theory could be placed before the world in a really perfected form, it was necessary to get some independent evidence about the existence of this young actor Willie Hughes. If this could be once established, there could be no possible doubt about his identity with Mr W. H.; but otherwise the theory would fall to the ground. I put this forward very strongly to Cyril, who was a good deal annoyed at what he called my Philistine tone of mind, and indeed was rather bitter upon the subject. However, I made him promise that in his own interest he would not publish his discovery till he had put the whole matter beyond the reach of doubt; and for weeks and weeks we searched the registers of City churches, the Alleyn MSS. at Dulwich, the Record Office, the papers of the Lord Chamberlain—everything, in fact, that we thought might contain some allusion to Willie Hughes. We discovered nothing, of course, and every day the existence of Willie Hughes seemed to me to become more problematical. Cyril was in a dreadful state, and used to go over the whole

question day after day, entreating me to believe; but I saw
the one flaw in the theory, and I refused to be convinced till
the actual existence of Willie Hughes, a boy-actor of
Elizabethan days, had been placed beyond the reach of doubt
or cavil.

"One day Cyril left town to stay with his grandfather, I
thought at the time, but I afterwards heard from Lord
Crediton that this was not the case; and about a fortnight
afterwards I received a telegram from him, handed in at
Warwick, asking me to be sure to come and dine with him
that evening at eight o'clock. When I arrived, he said to me
'The only apostle who did not deserve proof was S.
Thomas, and S. Thomas was the only apostle who got it.' I
asked him what he meant. He answered that he had not
merely been able to establish the existence in the sixteenth
century of a boy-actor of the name of Willie Hughes, but to
prove by the most conclusive evidence that he was the Mr
W. H. of the Sonnets. He would not tell me anything more
at the time; but after dinner he solemnly produced the picture
I showed you, and told me that he had discovered it by the
merest chance nailed to the side of an old chest that he had
bought at a farmhouse in Warwickshire. The chest itself,
which was a very fine example of Elizabeth work, he had, of
course, brought with him, and in the centre of the front panel
the initials W. H. were undoubtedly carved. It was this
monogram that had attracted his attention, and he told me
that it was not till he had had the chest in his possession for
several days that he had thought of making any careful
examination of the inside. One morning, however, he saw
that one of the sides of the chest was much thicker than the
other, and looking more closely, he discovered that a framed
panel picture was clamped against it. On taking it out, he
found it was the picture that is now lying on the sofa. It was
very dirty, and covered with mould; but he managed to clean

it, and, to his great joy, saw that he had fallen by mere chance on the one thing for which he had been looking. Here was an authentic portrait of Mr W. H., with his hand resting on the dedicatory page of the Sonnets, and on the frame itself could be faintly seen the name of the young man written in black uncial letters on a faded gold ground, 'Master Will. Hews.'

"Well, what was I to say? It never occurred to me for a moment that Cyril Graham was playing a trick on me, or that he was trying to prove his theory by means of a forgery."

"But is it a forgery?" I asked.

"Of course it is," said Erskine. "It is a very good forgery; but it is a forgery none the less. I thought at the time that Cyril was rather calm about the whole matter; but I remember he more than once told me that he himself required no proof of the kind, and that he thought the theory complete without it. I laughed at him, and told him that without it the theory would fall to the ground, and I warmly congratulated him on the marvellous discovery. We then arranged that the picture should be etched or facsimiled, and placed as the frontispiece to Cyril's edition of the Sonnets; and for three months we did nothing but go over each poem line by line, till we had settled every difficulty of text or meaning. One unlucky day I was in a print-shop in Holborn, when I saw upon the counter some extremely beautiful drawings in silver-point. I was so attracted by them that I bought them; and the proprietor of the place, a man called Rawlings, told me that they were done by a young painter of the name of Edward Merton, who was very clever, but as poor as a church mouse. I went to see Merton some days afterwards, having got his address from the print-seller, and found a pale, interesting young man, with a rather common-looking wife—his model, as I subsequently learned. I told him how much I admired his drawings, at which he seemed very pleased, and I asked him if he would show me some of his other work. As we were looking over a portfolio, full of really very lovely things,—for Merton had a most delicate and delightful touch,—I suddenly caught sight of a drawing of the picture of Mr W. H. There was no doubt whatever about it. It was almost a facsimile—the only difference being that the two masks of Tragedy and Comedy were not suspended from the marble table as they are in the picture, but were lying on the floor at the young man's feet. 'Where on earth did you get that?' I said. He grew rather confused, and said—'Oh, that is nothing. I did not know it was in this portfolio. It is not a thing of any value.' 'It is what you did for Mr Cyril Graham,' exclaimed his wife; 'and if this gentleman wishes to buy it, let him have it.' 'For Mr Cyril Graham?' I repeated. 'Did you paint the picture of Mr W. H.?' 'I don't understand what you mean,' he answered, growing very red. Well, the whole thing was quite dreadful. The wife let it all out. I gave her five pounds when I was going away. I can't bear to think of it now; but of course I was furious. I went off at once to Cyril's chambers, waited there for three hours before he came in, with that horrid lie staring me in the face, and told him I had discovered his forgery. He grew very pale, and said—'I did it purely for your sake. You would not be convinced in any other way. It does not affect the truth of the theory.' 'The truth of the theory!' I exclaimed; 'the less we talk about that the better. You never even believed in it yourself. If you had, you would not have committed a forgery to prove it.' High words passed between us; we had a fearful quarrel. I daresay I was unjust. The next morning he was dead."

"Dead!" I cried.

"Yes; he shot himself with a revolver. Some of the blood splashed upon the frame of the picture, just where the name had been painted. By the time I arrived—his servant had sent for me at once—the police were already there. He had left a letter for me, evidently written in the greatest agitation and distress of mind."

"What was in it?" I asked.

"Oh, that he believed absolutely in Willie Hughes; that the forgery of the picture had been done simply as a concession to me, and did not in the slightest degree invalidate the truth of the theory; and that in order to show me how firm and flawless his faith in the whole thing was, he was going to offer his life as a sacrifice to the secret of the Sonnets. It was a foolish, mad letter. I remember he ended by saying that he intrusted to me the Willie Hughes theory, and that it was for me to present it to the world, and to unlock the secret of Shakespeare's heart."

"It is a most tragic story," I cried; "but why have you not carried out his wishes?"

Erskine shrugged his shoulders. "Because it is a perfectly unsound theory from beginning to end," he answered.

"My dear Erskine," I said, getting up from my seat, "you are entirely wrong about the whole matter. It is the only perfect key to Shakespeare's Sonnets that has ever been made. It is complete in every detail. I believe in Willie Hughes."

"Don't say that," said Erskine, gravely; "I believe there is something fatal about the idea, and intellectually there is nothing to be said for it. I have gone into the whole matter, and I assure you the theory is entirely fallacious. It is plausible up to a certain point. Then it stops. For heaven's sake, my dear boy, don't take up the subject of Willie Hughes. You will break your heart over it."

"Erskine," I answered, "it is your duty to give this theory to the world. If you will not do it, I will. By keeping it back you wrong the memory of Cyril Graham, the youngest and the most splendid of all the martyrs of literature. I entreat you to do him justice. He died for this thing,—don't let his death be in vain."

Erskine looked at me in amazement. "You are carried away by the sentiment of the whole story," he said. "You forget that a thing is not necessarily true because a man dies for it. I was devoted to Cyril Graham. His death was a horrible blow to me. I did not recover it for years. I don't think I have ever recovered it. But Willie Hughes? There is nothing in the idea of Willie Hughes. No such person ever existed. As for bringing the whole thing before the world— the world thinks that Cyril Graham shot himself by accident. The only proof of his suicide was contained in the letter to me, and of this letter the public never heard anything. To the present day Lord Crediton thinks that the whole thing was accidental."

"Cyril Graham sacrificed his life to a great idea," I answered; "and if you will not tell of his martyrdom, tell at least of his faith."

"His faith," said Erskine, "was fixed in a thing that was false, in a thing that was unsound, in a thing that no Shakespearian scholar would accept for a moment. The theory would be laughed at. Don't make a fool of yourself, and don't follow a trail that leads nowhere. You start by assuming the existence of the very person whose existence is the thing to be proved. Besides, everybody knows that the Sonnets were addressed to Lord Pembroke. The matter is settled once for all."

"The matter is not settled!" I exclaimed. "I will take up the theory where Cyril Graham left it, and I will prove to the world that he was right."

"Silly boy!" said Erskine. "Go home: it is after two, and don't think about Willie Hughes any more. I am sorry I told you anything about it, and very sorry indeed that I should have converted you to a thing in which I don't believe."

"You have given me the key to the greatest mystery of modern literature," I answered; "and I shall not rest till I have made you recognise, till I have made everybody recognise, that Cyril Graham was the most subtle Shakespearian critic of our day."

As I walked home through St James's Park the dawn was just breaking over London. The white swans were lying asleep on the polished lake, and the gaunt Palace looked purple against the pale-green sky. I thought of Cyril Graham, and my eyes filled with tears.

II.

It was past twelve o'clock when I awoke, and the sun was streaming in through the curtains of my room in long slanting beams of dusty gold. I told my servant that I would be at home to no one; and after I had had a cup of chocolate and a *petit-pain*, I took down from the book-shelf my copy of Shakespeare's Sonnets, and began to go carefully through them. Every poem seemed to me to corroborate Cyril Graham's theory. I felt as if I had my hand upon Shakespeare's heart, and was counting each separate throb and pulse of passion. I thought of the wonderful boy-actor, and saw his face in every line.

Two sonnets, I remember, struck me particularly: they were the 53d and the 67th. In the first of these, Shakespeare, complimenting Willie Hughes on the versatility of his acting, on his wide range of parts, a range extending from Rosalind to Juliet and from Beatrice to Ophelia, says to him—

"What is your substance, whereof are you made,
That millions of strange shadows on you tend?

> Since every one hath, every one, one shade,
> And you, but one, can every shadow lend"—

lines that would be unintelligible if they were not addressed
to an actor, for the word "shadow" had in Shakespeare's day
a technical meaning connected with the stage. "The best in
this kind are but shadows," says Theseus of the actors in the
"Midsummer Night's Dream," and there are many similar
allusions in the literature of the day. These sonnets evidently
belonged to the series in which Shakespeare discusses the
nature of the actor's art, and of the strange and rare
temperament that is essential to the perfect stage-player.
"How is it," says Shakespeare to Willie Hughes, "that you
have so many personalities?" and then he goes on to point
out that his beauty is such that it seems to realise every form
and phase of fancy, to embody each dream of the creative
imagination—an idea that is still further expanded in the
sonnet that immediately follows, where, beginning with the
fine thought,

> "O, how much more doth beauty beauteous seem
> By that sweet ornament which *truth* doth give!"

Shakespeare invites us to notice how the truth of acting, the
truth of visible presentation on the stage, adds to the wonder
of poetry, giving life to its loveliness, and actual reality to its
ideal form. And yet, in the 67th sonnet, Shakespeare calls
upon Willie Hughes to abandon the stage with its
artificiality, its false mimic life of painted face and unreal
costume, its immoral influences and suggestions, its
remoteness from the true world of noble action and sincere
utterance.

> "Ah! wherefore with infection he live,

And with his present grace impiety,
That sin by him advantage should achieve,
And lace itself with his society?
Why should false painting imitate his cheek
And steal dead seeming of his living hue?
Why should poor beauty indirectly seek
Roses of shadow, since his rose is true?"

It may seem strange that so great a dramatist as Shakespeare, who realised his own perfection as an artist and his humanity as a man on the ideal plane of stage-writing and stage-playing, should have written in these terms about the theatre; but we must remember that in Sonnets cx. and cxi. Shakespeare shows us that he too was wearied of the world of puppets, and full of shame at having made himself "a motley to the view." The 111th Sonnet is especially bitter:—

"O, for my sake do you with Fortune chide
The guilty goddess of my harmful deeds,
That did not better for my life provide
Than public means which public manners breeds.
Thence comes it that my name receives a brand,
And almost thence my nature is subdued
To what it works in, like the dyer's hand:
Pity me, then, and wish I were renewed"—

and there are many signs elsewhere of the same feeling, signs familiar to all real students of Shakespeare.

One point puzzled me immensely as I read the Sonnets, and it was days before I struck on the true interpretation, which indeed Cyril Graham himself seems to have missed. I could not understand how it was that Shakespeare set so high a value on his young friend marrying. He himself had married young, and the result had been unhappiness, and it was not likely that he would have asked Willie Hughes to commit the same error. The boy-player of Rosalind had

nothing to gain from marriage, or from the passions of real
life. The early sonnets, with their strange entreaties to have
children, seemed to me a jarring note. The explanation of the
mystery came on me quite suddenly, and I found it in the
curious dedication. It will be remembered that the dedication
runs as follows:—

"TO • THE • ONLIE • BEGETTER • OF •
THESE • INSUING • SONNETS •
MR W. H. • ALL • HAPPINESSE •
AND • THAT • ETERNITIE •
PROMISED • BY •
OUR • EVER-LIVING • POET •
WISHETH •
THE • WELL-WISHING •
ADVENTURER • IN •
SETTING •
FORTH.

T. T."

Some scholars have supposed that the word "begetter" in
this dedication means simply the procurer of the Sonnets for
Thomas Thorpe the publisher; but this view is now generally
abandoned, and the highest authorities are quite agreed that it
is to be taken in the sense of inspirer, the metaphor being
drawn from the analogy of physical life. Now I saw that the
same metaphor was used by Shakespeare himself all through
the poems, and this set me on the right track. Finally I made
my great discovery. The marriage that Shakespeare proposes
for Willie Hughes is the "marriage with his Muse," an
expression which is definitely put forward in the 82d
Sonnet, where, in the bitterness of his heart at the defection
of the boy-actor for whom he had written his greatest parts,

and whose beauty had indeed suggested them, he opens his complaint by saying—

"I'll grant thou were not married to my Muse."

The children he begs him to beget are no children of flesh and blood, but more immortal children of undying fame. The whole cycle of the early sonnets is simply Shakespeare's invitation to Willie Hughes to go upon the stage and become a player. How barren and profitless a thing, he says, is this beauty of yours if it be not used:

"When the forty winters shall besiege thy brow,
And dig deep trenches in thy beauty's field,
Thy youth's proud livery, so gazed on now,
Will be a tattered weed, of small worth held:
Then being asked where all thy beauty lies,
Where all the treasure of thy lusty days,
To say, within thine own deep-sunken eyes,
Were an all-eating shame and thriftless praise."

You must create something in art: my verse "is thine, and *born* of thee;" only listen to me, and I will "*bring forth* eternal numbers to outlive long date," and you shall people with forms of your own image the imaginary world of the stage. These children that you beget, he continues, will not wither away, as mortal children do, but you shall live in them and in my plays: do but

"Make thee another self, for love of me,
That beauty still may live in thine or thee!"

I collected all the passages that seemed to me to corroborate this view, and they produced a strong impression on me, and showed me how complete Cyril

Graham's theory really was. I also saw that it was quite easy
to separate those lines in which he speaks of the Sonnets
themselves from those in which he speaks of his great
dramatic work. This was a point that had been entirely
overlooked by all critics up to Cyril Graham's day. And yet
it was one of the most important points in the whole series of
poems. To the Sonnets Shakespeare was more or less
indifferent. He did not wish to rest his fame on them. They
were to him his "slight Muse," as he calls them, and
intended, as Meres tells us, for private circulation only
among a few, a very few, friends. Upon the other hand he
was extremely conscious of the high artistic value of his
plays, and shows a noble self-reliance upon his dramatic
genius. When he says to Willie Hughes:

> "But thy eternal summer shall not fade,
> Nor lose possession of that fair thou owest;
> Nor shall Death brag thou wander'st in his shade,
> When in *eternal lines* to time thou growest;
>> So long as men can breathe or eyes can see,
>> So long lives this and this gives life to thee;"—

the expression "eternal lines" clearly alludes to one of his
plays that he was sending him at the time, just as the
concluding couplet points to his confidence in the probability
of his plays being always acted. In his address to the
Dramatic Muse (Sonnets c. and ci.), we find the same
feeling.

> "Where art thou, Muse, that thou forget'st so long
> To speak of that which gives thee all thy might?
> Spends thou thy fury on some worthless song,
> Darkening thy power to lend base subjects light?"

he cries, and he then proceeds to reproach the mistress of Tragedy and Comedy for her "neglect of Truth in Beauty dyed," and says—

> "Because he needs no praise, wilt thou be dumb?
> Excuse not silence so; for 't lies in thee
> To make him much outlive a gilded tomb,
> And to be praised of ages yet to be.
>   Then do thy office, Muse; I teach thee how
>   To make him seem long hence as he shows now."

It is, however, perhaps in the 55th Sonnet that Shakespeare gives to this idea its fullest expression. To imagine that the "powerful rhyme" of the second line refers to the sonnet itself, is to entirely mistake Shakespeare's meaning. It seemed to me that it was extremely likely, from the general character of the sonnet, that a particular play was meant, and that the play was none other but "Romeo and Juliet."

> "Not marble, nor the gilded monuments
> Of princes, shall outlive this powerful rhyme;
> But you shall shine more bright in these contents
> Than unswept stone besmeared with sluttish time.
> When wasteful wars shall statues overturn,
> And broils root out the work of masonry,
> Not Mars his sword nor war's quick fire shall burn
> The living record of your memory.
> 'Gainst death and all-oblivious enmity
> Shall you pace forth; your praise shall still find room
> Even in the eyes of all posterity
> That wear this world out to the ending doom.
>   So, till the judgment that yourself arise,
>   You live in this, and dwell in lovers' eyes."

It was also extremely suggestive to note how here as elsewhere Shakespeare promised Willie Hughes immortality in a form that appealed to men's eyes—that is to say, in a spectacular form, in a play that is to be looked at.

For two weeks I worked hard at the Sonnets, hardly ever going out, and refusing all invitations. Every day I seemed to be discovering something new, and Willie Hughes became to me a kind of spiritual presence, an ever-dominant personality. I could almost fancy that I saw him standing in the shadow of my room, so well had Shakespeare drawn him, with his golden hair, his tender flower-like grace, his dreamy deep-sunken eyes, his delicate mobile limbs, and his white lily hands. His very name fascinated me. Willie Hughes! Willie Hughes! How musically it sounded! Yes; who else but he could have been the master-mistress of Shakespeare's passion,[1] the lord of his love to whom he was bound in vassalage,[2] the delicate minion of pleasure,[3] the rose of the whole world,[4] the herald of the spring[5] decked in the proud livery of youth,[6] the lovely boy whom it was sweet music to hear,[7] and whose beauty was the very raiment of Shakespeare's heart,[8] as it was the keystone of his dramatic power? How bitter now seemed the whole tragedy of his desertion and his shame!—shame that he made sweet and lovely[9] by the mere magic of his personality, but that was none the less shame. Yet as Shakespeare forgave him, should not we forgive him also? I did not care to pry into the mystery of his sin.

His abandonment of Shakespeare's theatre was a different matter, and I investigated it at great length. Finally I came to the conclusion that Cyril Graham had been wrong in regarding the rival dramatist of the 80th Sonnet as Chapman. It was obviously Marlowe who was alluded to. At the time the Sonnets were written, such an expression as "the proud full sail of his great verse" could not have been used of Chapman's work, however applicable it might have been to the style of his later Jacobean plays. No: Marlowe was clearly the rival dramatist of whom Shakespeare spoke in such laudatory terms; and that

"Affable familiar ghost
Which nightly gulls him with intelligence,"

was the Mephistopheles of his Doctor Faustus. No doubt, Marlowe was fascinated by the beauty and grace of the boy-actor, and lured him away from the Blackfriars' Theatre, that he might play the Gaveston of his "Edward II." That Shakespeare had the legal right to retain Willie Hughes in his own company is evident from Sonnet lxxxvii., where he says:—

"Farewell! thou art too dear for my possessing,
And like enough thou know'st thy estimate:
The *charter of thy worth* gives thee releasing;
My *bonds* in thee are all determinate.
For how do I hold thee but by thy granting?
And for that riches where is my deserving?
The cause of this fair gift in me is wanting,
And so my patent back again is serving.
Thyself thou gavest, thy own work then not knowing,
Or me, to whom thou gavest it, else mistaking;
So thy great gift, upon misprision growing,
Comes none again, on better judgment making.
    This have I had thee, as a dream doth flatter,
    In sleep a king, but waking no such matter."

But him whom he could not hold by love, he would not hold by force. Willie Hughes became a member of Lord Pembroke's company, and, perhaps in the open yard of the Red Bull Tavern, played the part of King Edward's delicate minion. On Marlowe's death, he seems to have returned to Shakespeare, who, whatever his fellow-partners may have thought of the matter, was not slow to forgive the wilfulness and treachery of the young actor.

How well, too, had Shakespeare drawn the temperament of the stage-player! Willie Hughes was one of those

"That do not do the thing they most do show,
Who, moving others, are themselves as stone."

He could act love, but could not feel it, could mimic passion without realising it.

"In many's looks the false heart's history
Is writ in moods and frowns and wrinkles strange,"

but with Willie Hughes it was not so. "Heaven," says Shakespeare, in a sonnet of mad idolatry—

"Heaven in thy creation did decree
That in thy face sweet love should ever dwell;
Whate'er thy thoughts or thy heart's workings be,
Thy looks hold nothing thence but sweetness tell."

In his "inconstant mind" and his "false heart," it was easy to recognise the insincerity and treachery that somehow seem inseparable from the artistic nature, as in his love of praise, that desire for immediate recognition that characterises all actors. And yet, more fortunate in this than other actors, Willie Hughes was to know something of immortality. Inseparably connected with Shakespeare's plays, he was to live in them.

"Your name from hence immortal life shall have,
Though I, once gone, to all the world must die:
The earth can yield me but a common grave,
When you entombed in men's eyes shall lie.

Your monument shall be my gentle verse,
Which eyes not yet created shall o'er-read,
And tongues to be your being shall rehearse
When all the breathers of this world are dead."

There were endless allusions, also, to Willie Hughes's power over his audience,—the "gazers," as Shakespeare call them; but perhaps the most perfect description of his wonderful mastery over dramatic art was in "The Lover's Complaint," where Shakespeare says of him:—

"In him a plentitude of subtle matter,
Applied to cautels, all strange forms receives,
Of burning blushes, or of weeping water,
Or swooning paleness; and he take and leaves,
In either's aptness, as it best deceives,
To blush at speeches rank, to weep at woes,
Or to turn white and swoon at tragic shows.
    • • • •
So on the tip of his subduing tongue,
All kind of arguments and questions deep,
All replication prompt and reason strong,
For his advantage still did wake and sleep,
To make the weeper laugh, and laugher weep.
  He had the dialect and the different skill,
  Catching all passions in his craft of will."

Once I thought that I had really found Willie Hughes in Elizabethan literature. In a wonderfully graphic account of the last days of the great Earl of Essex, his chaplain, Thomas Knell, tells us that the night before the Earl died, "he called William Hewes, which was his musician, to play upon the virginals and to sing. 'Play,' said he, 'my song, Will Hewes, and I will sing it myself.' So he did it most joyfully, not as the howling swan, which, still looking down, waileth her end, but as a sweek lark, lifting up his hands and casting up his eyes to his God, with this mounted the crystal skies, and reached with his unwearied tongue the top of highest heavens." Surely the boy who played on the virginals to the dying father of Sidney's Stella was none other but the Will Hews to whom Shakespeare dedicated the Sonnets, and whom he tells us was himself sweet "music to hear." Yet Lord Essex died in 1576, when Shakespeare himself was but twelve years of age. It was impossible that his musician could been the Mr W. H. of the Sonnets. Perhaps Shakespeare's young friend was the son of the player upon the virginals? It was at least something to have discovered that Will Hews was an Elizabethan name. Indeed the name Hews seemed to have been closely connected with music and the stage. The first English actress was the lovely Margaret Hews, whom Prince Rupert so madly loved. What more probable than that between her and Lord Essex's musician had come the boy-actor of Shakespeare's plays? But the proofs, the links—where were they? Alas! I could not find them. It seemed to me that I was always on the brink of absolute verification, but that I could never really attain to it.

From Willie Hughes's life I soon passed to thought of his death. I used to wonder what had been his end.

Perhaps he had been one of those English actors who in 1604 went across sea to Germany and played before the great Duke Henry Julius of Brunswick, himself a dramatist of no mean order, and at the Court of that Elector of Brandenburg, who was so enamoured of beauty that he was said to have bought for his weight in amber the young son of a travelling Greek merchant, and to have given pageants in honour of his slave all through that dreadful famine year of 1606-7, when the people died of hunger in the very streets of the town, and for the space of seven months there was no rain. We know at any rate that "Romeo and Juliet" was

brought out at Dresden in 1613, along with "Hamlet" and
"King Lear," and it was surely to none other than Willie
Hughes that in 1615 the death-mask of Shakespeare was
brought by the hand of one of the suite of the English
ambassador, pale token of the passing away of the great poet
who had so dearly loved him. Indeed there would have been
something peculiarly fitting in the idea that the boy-actor,
whose beauty had been so vital an element in the realism and
romance of Shakespeare's art, should have been the first to
have brought to Germany the seed of the new culture, and
was in his way the precursor of that *Aufklarung* or
Illumination of the eighteenth century, that splendid
movement which, though begun by Lessing and Herder, and
brought to its full and perfect issue by Goethe, was in no
small part helped on by another actor—Friedrich
Schroeder—who awoke the popular consciousness, and by
means of the feigned passions and mimetic methods of the
stage showed the intimate, the vital, connection between life
and literature. If this was so,—and there was certainly no
evidence against it,—it was not improbable that Willie
Hughes was one of those English comedians (*mimæ quidam
ex Britannia*, as the old chronicle calls them), who were slain
at Nuremberg in a sudden uprising of the people, and were
secretly buried in a little vineyard outside the city by some
young men "who had found pleasure in their performances,
and of whom some had sought to be instructed in the
mysteries of the new art." Certainly no more fitting place
could there be for him to whom Shakespeare said, "thou art
all my art," than this little vineyard outside the city walls.
For was it not from the sorrows of Dionysos that Tragedy
sprang? Was not the light laughter of Comedy, with its
careless merriment and quick replies, first heard on the lips
of the Sicilian vine-dresser? Nay, did not the purple and red
stain of the wine-froth on face and limbs give the first

suggestion of the charm and fascination of disguise—the desire for self-concealment, the sense of the value of objectivity thus showing itself in the rude beginnings of the art? At any rate, where he lay—whether in the little vineyard at the gate of the Gothic town, or in some dim London churchyard amidst the roar and bustle of our great city—no gorgeous monument marked his resting-place. His true tomb, as Shakespeare saw, was the poet's verse, his true monument the permanence of the drama. So had it been with others whose beauty had given a new creative impulse to their age. The ivory body of the Bithynian slave rots in the green ooze of the Nile, and on the yellow hills of the Cerameicus is strewn the dust of the young Athenian; but Antinous lives in sculpture, and Charmides in philosophy.

III.

After three weeks had elapsed, I determined to make a strong appeal to Erskine to do justice to the memory of Cyril Graham, and to give to the world his marvellous interpretation of the Sonnets—the only interpretation that thoroughly explained the problem. I have not any copy of my letter, I regret to say, nor have I been able to lay my hand upon the original; but I remember that I went over the whole ground, and covered sheets of paper with passionate reiteration of the arguments and proofs that my study had suggested to me. It seemed to me that I was not merely restoring Cyril Graham to his proper place in literary history, but rescuing the honour of Shakespeare himself from the tedious memory of a commonplace intrigue. I put into the letter all my enthusiasm. I put into the letter all my faith.

No sooner, in fact, had I sent it off than a curious reaction came over me. It seemed to me that I had given away my capacity for belief in the Willie Hughes theory of the Sonnets, that something had gone out of me, as it were, and that I was perfectly indifferent to the whole subject. What was it that had happened? It is difficult to say. Perhaps, by finding perfect expression for a passion, I had exhausted the passion itself. Emotional forces, like the forces of physical life, have their positive limitations. Perhaps the mere effort to convert any one to a theory involves some form of renunciation of the power of credence. Perhaps I was simply tired of the whole thing, and, my enthusiasm having burnt out, my reason was left to its own unimpassioned judgment. However it came about, and I cannot pretend to explain it, there was no doubt that Willie Hughes suddenly became to me a mere myth, an idle dream, the boyish fancy of a young man who, like most ardent spirits, was more anxious to convince others than to be himself convinced.

As I had said some very unjust and bitter things to Erskine in my letter, I determined to go and see him at once, and to make my apologies to him for my behaviour. Accordingly, the next morning I drove down to Birdcage Walk, and found Erskine sitting in his library, with the forged picture of Willie Hughes in front of him.

"My dear Erskine!" I cried, "I have come to apologise to you."

"To apologise to me?" he said. "What for?"

"For my letter," I answered.

"You have nothing to regret in your letter," he said. "On the contrary, you have done me the greatest service in your power. You have shown me that Cyril Graham's theory is perfectly sound."

"You don't mean to say that you believe in Willie Hughes?" I exclaimed.

"Why not?" he rejoined. "You have proved the thing to me. Do you think I cannot estimate the value of evidence."

"But there is no evidence at all," I groaned, sinking into a chair. "When I wrote to you I was under the influence of a perfectly silly enthusiasm. I had been touched by the story of Cyril Graham's death, fascinated by his romantic theory, enthralled by the wonder and novelty of the whole idea. I see now that the theory is based on a delusion. The only evidence for the existence of Willie Hughes is that picture in front of you, and the picture is a forgery. Don't be carried away by mere sentiment in this matter. Whatever romance may have to say about the Willie Hughes theory, reason is dead against it."

"I don't understand you," said Erskine, looking at me in amazement. "Why, you yourself have convinced me by your letter that Willie Hughes is an absolute reality. Why have you changed your mind? Or is all that you have been saying to me merely a joke?"

"I cannot explain it to you," I rejoined, "but I see now that there is really nothing to be said in favour of Cyril Graham's interpretation. The sonnets are addressed to Lord Pembroke. For heaven's sake don't waste your time in a foolish attempt to discover a young Elizabethan actor who never existed, and to make a phantom puppet the centre of the great cycle of Shakespeare's Sonnets."

"I see that you don't understand the theory," he replied.

"My dear Erskine," I cried, "not understand it! Why, I feel as if I had invented it. Surely my letter shows you that I not merely went into the whole matter, but that I contributed proofs of every kind. The one flaw in the theory is that it presupposes the existence of the person whose existence is the subject of dispute. If we grant that there was in Shakespeare's company a young actor of the name of Willie Hughes, it is not difficult to make him the object of the Sonnets. But as we know that there was no actor of this name in the company of the Globe Theatre, it is idle to pursue the investigation further."

"But that is exactly what we don't know," said Erskine. "It is quite true that his name does not occur in the list given in the first folio; but, as Cyril pointed out, that is rather a proof in favour of the existence of Willie Hughes than against it, if we remember his treacherous desertion of Shakespeare for a rival dramatist."

We argued the matter over for hours, but nothing that I could say could make Erskine surrender his faith in Cyril Graham's interpretation. He told me that he intended to devote his life to proving the theory, and that he was determined to do justice to Cyril Graham's memory. I entreated him, laughed at him, begged of him, but it was of no use. Finally we parted, not exactly in anger, but certainly with a shadow between us. He thought me shallow, I thought him foolish. When I called on him again, his servant told me that he had gone to Germany.

Two years afterwards, as I was going into my club, the hall-porter handed me a letter with a foreign postmark. It was from Erskine, and written at the Hotel d'Angleterre, Cannes. When I had read it I was filled with horror, though I did not quite believe that he would be so mad as to carry his resolve into execution. The gist of the letter was that he had tried in every way to verify the Willie Hughes theory, and had failed, and that as Cyril Graham had given his life for this theory, he himself had determined to give his own life also to the same cause. The concluding words of the letter were these: "I still believe in Willie Hughes; and by the time you receive this, I shall have died by my own hand for Willie Hughes's sake: for his sake, and for the sake of Cyril Graham, whom I drove to his death by my shallow scepticism and ignorant lack of faith. The truth was once revealed to you, and you rejected it. It comes to you now stained with the blood of two lives,—do not turn away from it."

It was a horrible moment. I felt sick with misery, and yet I could not believe it. To die for one's theological beliefs is the worse use a man can make of his life, but to die for a literary theory! It seemed impossible.

I looked at the date. The letter was a week old. Some unfortunate chance had prevented my going to the club for several days, or I might have got it in time to save him. Perhaps it was not too late. I drove off to my rooms, packed up my things, and started by the night-mail from Charing Cross. The journey was intolerable. I thought I would never arrive.

As soon as I did I drove to the Hotel d'Angleterre. They told me that Erskine had been buried two days before, in the English cemetery. There was something horribly grotesque about the whole tragedy. I said all kinds of wild things, and the people in the hall looked curiously at me.

Suddenly Lady Erskine, in deep mourning, passed across the vestibule. When she saw me she came up to me, murmured something about her poor son, and burst into tears. I led her into her sitting-room. An elderly gentleman was there waiting for her. It was the English doctor.

We talked a great deal about Erskine, but I said nothing about his motive for committing suicide. It was evident that he had not told his mother anything about the reason that had driven him to so fatal, so mad an act. Finally Lady Erskine rose and said, "George left you something as a memento. It was a thing he prized very much. I will get it for you."

As soon as she had left the room I turned to the doctor and said, "What a dreadful shock it must have been to Lady Erskine! I wonder that she bears it as well as she does."

"Oh, she knew for months past that it was coming," he answered.

"Knew it for months past!" I cried. "But why didn't she stop him? Why didn't she have him watched? He must have been mad."

The doctor stared at me. "I don't know what you mean," he said.

"Well," I cried, "if a mother knows that her son is going to commit suicide——"

"Suicide!" he answered. "Poor Erskine did not commit suicide. He died of consumption. He came here to die. The moment I saw him I knew that there was no hope. One lung was almost gone, and the other was very affected. Three days before he died he asked me was there any hope. I told him frankly that there was none, and that he had only a few days to live. He wrote some letters, and was quite resigned, retaining his senses to the last."

At that moment Lady Erskine entered the room with the fatal picture of Willie Hughes in her hand. "When George was dying he begged me to give you this," she said. As I took it from her, her tears fell on my hand.

The picture hangs now in my library, where it is very much admired by my artistic friends. They have decided that it is not a Clouet, but an Ouvry. I have never cared to tell them its true history. But sometimes, when I look at it, I think that there is really a great deal to be said for the Willie Hughes theory of Shakespeare's Sonnets.

NOTES

[1]Sonnet xx. 2.
[2]Sonnet xxvi. 1.
[3]Sonnet cxxvi. 9.
[4]Sonnet cix. 14.
[5]Sonnet i. 10.

[6]Sonnet ii. 3.
[7]Sonnet viii. 1.
[8]Sonnet xxii. 6.
[9]Sonnet xcv. 1.

PROOFS OF HOLY WRIT

Rudyard Kipling

They seated themselves in the heavy chairs on the pebbled floor beneath the eaves of the summer-house by the orchard. A table between them carried the wine and glasses, and a packet of papers, with pen and ink. The larger man of the two, his doublet unbuttoned, his broad face blotched and scarred, puffed a little as he came to rest. The other picked an apple from the grass, bit it, and went on with the thread of the talk that they must have carried out of doors with them.

"But why waste time fighting atomies who do not come up to your belly-button, Ben?" he asked.

"It breathes me—it breathes me, between bouts! *You'd* be better for a tussle or two."

"But not to spend mind and verse on 'em. What was Dekker to you? Ye knew he'd strike back—and hard."

"He and Marston had been baiting me like dogs . . . about my trade as they called it, though it was only my

cursed stepfather's. 'Bricks and mortar,' Dekker said, and
'hodman.' And he mocked my face. 'Twas clean as curds in
my youth. This humour has come on me since."

"Ah! 'Every man and his humour'? But why did ye not
have at Dekker in peace—over the sack, as you do at me?"

"Because I'd have drawn on him—and he's no more
worth a hanging than Gabriel. Setting aside what he wrote of
me, too, the hireling dog has merit of a sort. His
Shoemaker's Holiday. Hey? Though my *Bartlemy Fair*,
when 'tis presented, will furnish out three of it and——"

"Ride all the easier. I have suffered two readings of it
already. It creaks like an overloaded haywain', the other cut
in. 'You give too much.'"

Ben smiled loftily and went on. "But I'm glad I lashed
him in my *Poetaster* for all I've worked with him since.
How comes it that I've never fought with thee, Will?"

"First, Behemoth" the other drawled, "it needs two to
engender any sort of iniquity. Second, the betterment of this
present age—and the next, maybe—lies, in chief, on our
four shoulders. If the Pillars of the Temple fall out, Nature,
Art, and Learning come to a stand. Last, I am not yet ass
enough to hawk up my private spites before groundlings.
What do the Court, citizens or 'prentices give for thy
fallings-out or fallings-in with Dekker—or the Grand
Devil?"

"They should be taught, then—taught."

"Always *that*? What's your commission to enlighten us?"

"My own learning which I heaped up, lifelong, at my
own pains. My assured knowledge, also, of my craft and
art. I'll suffer no man's mock or malice on it."

"The one sure road to mockery."

"I deny nothing of my brain-store to my lines. I—I build
up my own works throughout."

"Yet when Dekker cries 'hodman' y'are not content."

Ben half-heaved in his chair. "I'll owe you a beating for that when I'm thinner. Meantime, here's on account, I say, I build upon my own foundations; devising and perfecting my own plots; adorning 'em justly as fits time, place and action. In all of which you sin damnably. I set no landward principalities on sea-beaches."

"They pay their penny for pleasure—not learning," Will answered above the apple-core.

"Penny or tester, you owe 'em justice. In the facture of plays—nay, listen, Will—at all points they must be dressed historically—*teres atque rotundus*—in ornament and temper. As my *Sejanus*, of which the mob was unworthy."

Here Will made a doleful face, and echoed. "Unworthy! I was—what did I play, Ben, in that long weariness. Some most grievous ass."

"The part of Caius Silius," said Ben, stiffly.

Will laughed aloud. "True. 'Indeed that place *was* not my sphere.'"

It must have been a quotation, for Ben winced a little, ere he recovered himself and went on: "Also my *Alchemist* which the world in part apprehends. The main of its learning is necessarily yet hid from 'em. To come to your works, Will——"

"I am a sinner on all sides. The drink's at your elbow."

"Confession shall not save ye—bribery." Ben filled his glass. "Sooner than labour the right cold heat to devise your own plots, you filch, botch, and clap 'em together out o' ballads, broadsheets, old wives' tales, chapbooks——"

Will nodded with complete satisfaction. "Say on," quoth he.

"'Tis so with nigh all yours. I've known honester jackdaws. And whom among the learned do ye deceive? Reckoning up those—forty is it?—your plays you've misbegot, there's not six which have not plots common as Moorditch."

"Ye're out, Ben. There's not one. My *Love's Labour* (how I came to write it, I know not) is nearest to lawful issue. My *Tempest* (how I came to write *that*, I know) is, in some part, my own stuff. Of the rest, I stand guilty. Bastards all!"

"And no shame?"

"None! Our business must be fitted with parts hot and hot—and the boys are more trouble than the men. Give me the bones of any stuff, I'll cover 'em as quickly as any. But to hatch new plots is to waste God's unreturning time like—" he chuckled, "like a hen."

"Yet see what ye miss! Invention next to Knowledge,— whence it proceeds, being the chief glory of Art——"

"Miss, say you? Dick Burbage—in my *Hamlet* that I botched for him when he had staled of our Kings? (Nobly he played it!) Was *he* a miss?"

Ere Ben could speak Will overbore him.

"And when poor Dick was at odds with the world in general and womenkind in special, I clapped him up my *Lear* for a vomit."

"An hotch-potch of passion, outrunning reason," was the verdict.

"Not altogether. Cast in a mould too large for any boards to bear (My fault!) Yet Dick evened it. And when he'd come out of his whoremongering aftermaths of repentance I served him my *Macbeth* to toughen him. Was that a miss?"

"I grant you, your *Macbeth* as nearest in spirit to my *Sejanus*; showing for example: 'How fortune plies her sports when she begins To practise 'em.' We'll see which of the two lives longest."

"Amen! I'll bear no malice among the worms."

A liveried serving-man, booted and spurred, led a saddlehorse through the gate into the orchard. At a sign from Will he tethered the beast to a tree, lurched aside and stretched on the grass. Ben, curious as a lizard, for all his bulk, wanted to know what it meant.

"There's a nosing Justice of the Peace lost in thee," Will returned. "Yon's a business I've neglected all this day for thy fat sake—and he by so much the drunker . . . Patience! It's all set out on the table. Have a care with the ink!"

Ben reached unsteadily for the packet of papers and read the superscription: "'To William Shakespeare, Gentleman, at this house of New Place in the town of Stratford, these— with diligence from M.S.' Why does the fellow withold his name? Or is it one of your women? I'll look."

Muzzy as he was, he opened and unfolded a mass of printed papers expertly enough.

"From the most learned divine, Miles Smith of Brazen Nose College," Will explained. "You know this business as well as I. The King has set all the scholars of England to make one Bible, which the Church shall be bound to, out of all the Bibles that men use."

"I knew." Ben could not lift his eyes from the printed page. "I'm more about the Court than you think. The learning of Oxford and Cambridge—'most noble and most equal,' as I have said—and Westminster, to sit upon a clutch of Bibles. Those 'ud be Geneva (my mother read to me out of it at her knee), Douai, Rheims, Coverdale, Matthews, the Bishops', the Great, and so forth."

"They are all set down on the page there—text against text. And you call me a botcher of old clothes?"

"Justly. But what's your concern with this botchery? To keep peace among the Divines? There's fifty of 'em at it as I've heard."

"I deal with but one. He came to know me when we played at Oxford—when the plague was too hot in London."

"I remember this Miles Smith now. Son of a butcher? Hey?" Ben grunted.

"Is it so?" was the quiet answer. "He was moved, he said, with some lines of mine in Dick's part. He said they were, to his godly apprehension, a parable, as it might be, of his reverend self, going down darkling to his tomb 'twixt cliffs of ice and iron."

"What lines? I know none of thine of that power. But in my *Sejanus*——"

"These were in my *Macbeth*. They lost nothing at Dick's mouth:

'Tomorrow and tomorrow and tomorrow
Creeps in this petty pace from day to day
To the last syllable of recorded time,
And all our yesterdays have lighted fools
The way to dusty death——'

or something in that sort. Condell writes 'em out fair for him, and tells him I am Justice of the Peace (wherein he lied) and *armiger*, which brings me within the pale of God's creatures and the Church. Little and little, then, this very reverend Miles Smith opens his mind to me. He and a half score others, his cloth, are cast to furbish up the Prophets— Isaiah to Malachi. In his opinion by what he'd heard, I had some skill in words, and he'd condescend——"

"How?" Ben barked. "Condescend?"

"Why not? He'd condescend to inquire o' me privily, when direct illumination lacked, for a tricking out of his words or the turn of some figure. For example"—Will pointed to the papers—"here be the first three verses of the

Sixtieth of Isaiah, and the nineteenth and twentieth of that same. Miles has been at a stand over 'em a week or more."

"They never called on me." Ben caressed lovingly the hand-pressed proofs on their lavish linen paper. "Here's the Latin atop and"—his thick forefinger ran down the slip—"some three—four—Englishings out of the other Bibles. They spare 'emselves nothing. Let's do it together. Will you have the Latin first?"

"Could I choke ye from that, Holofernes?"

Ben rolled forth, richly: "'*Surge, illumare, Jerusalem, quia venit lumen tuum, et gloria Domini super te orta est. Quia ecce tenebrae operient terram et caligo populos. Super te autem orietur Dominus, et gloria ejus in te videbitur. Et ambulabunt gentes in lumine tuo, et reges in splendore ortus tui.*' Er-hum? Think you to better that?"

"How have Smith's crew gone about it?"

"Thus." Ben read from the paper. "'Get thee up, O Jerusalem, and be bright, for thy light is at hand, and the glory of God has risen up upon thee.'"

"Up-pup-up!" Will stuttered, profanely.

Ben held on. "'See how darkness is upon the earth and the peoples thereof.'"

"That's no great stuff to put into Isaiah's mouth. And further, Ben?"

"'But on thee God shew light and on——' . . . or 'in' is it?" (Ben held the proof closer to the deep furrow at the bridge of his nose.) "'On thee shall His glory be manifest. So that all peoples shall walk in the light and the Kings in the glory of thy morning.'"

'It may be amended. Read me the Coverdale of it now. 'Tis on the same sheet—to the right, Ben.'

'Umm-umm. Coverdale saith. "And therefore get thee up be-times His glory shall be seen in thee. The Gentiles shall

come to thy light and the Kings to the brightness that springs
forth on thee.' But 'gentes' is, for the most part, 'peoples.'"

"Eh?" said Will, indifferently. "Art sure?"

This loosed an avalanche of instances from Ovid,
Quintilian, Terence, Columella, Seneca and others. Will took
no heed till the rush ceased, but stared into the orchard,
through the September haze. "Now give me the Douai and
Geneva for this 'Get thee up, O Jerusalem,'" said he at last.
"They'll be all there."

Ben referred to the proofs. "'Tis 'arise' in both," said
he. "'Arise and be bright' in Geneva. In the Douai 'tis 'Arise
and be illuminated.'"

"So? Give me the paper now." Will took it from his
companion, rose, and paced towards a tree in the orchard,
turning again, when he had reached it, by a well-worn track
through the grass, Ben leaned forward in his chair. The
other's free hand went up warningly.

"Quiet, man!" said he. "I wait on my Demon!" He fell
into the stage-stride of his art at that time, speaking to the air.

"How shall this open? 'Arise' No! 'Rise.' Yes. And
we'll have no weak coupling. 'Tis a call to a City! 'Rise—
shine' . . . Nor yet any schoolmaster's 'because'—because
Isaiah is not Holofernes. '*Rise—shine; for thy light is come,
and*——!'" He refreshed himself from the apple and the
proofs as he strode. "'And—and the glory of God!'—No!
'God's' over-short. We need the long roll here. "*And the
glory of the Lord is risen on thee.*" (Isaiah speaks the part.
We'll have it from his own lips.) What's next in Smith's
stuff? . . . 'See now'? Oh, vile—vile! . . . And Geneva hath
'Lo'? (Still, Ben! Still!) 'Lo' is better by all odds: but to
match the long roll of 'the Lord' we'll have *earth and—
and*— what's the colour and use of this cursed *caligo*,
Ben?— '*Et caligo populos.*'"

"'Mistiness' or, as in Pliny, 'blindness.' And further——"

"No-o . . . Maybe, though, *caligo* will piece out *tenebrae.* *'Quia ecce tenebrae operient terram et caligo populos.*' Nay! 'Shadow' and 'mist' are not men enough for this work . . . Blindness, did ye say, Ben? . . . The blackness of blindness atop of mere darkness? . . . By God, I've used it in my own stuff many times! 'Gross' searches it to the hilts! 'Darkness covers'—no, 'clokes' (short always). *'Darkness clokes the earth and gross—gross darkness the people*'! (But Isaiah's prophesying, with the storm behind him. Can ye not feel it, Ben? It must be 'shall')—*'Shall cloke the earth'* . . . The rest comes clearer. . . . 'But on thee God shall arise" . . . (Nay, that's sacrificing the Creator to the Creature!) *'But the Lord shall arise on thee,'* and—yes, we'll sound that 'thee' again—"and on thee shall"—No! . . . *'And His glory shall be seen on thee.'* Good!" He walked his beat a little in silence, mumbling the two verses before he mouthed them.

"I have it! Heark, Ben! *'Rise—shine; for thy light is come and the glory of the Lord is risen on thee. For, behold, darkness shall cloke the earth and gross darkness the people. But the Lord shall arise on thee and His glory shall be seen upon thee.'*"

"There's something not all amiss there," Ben conceded.

"My Demon never betrayed me yet, while I trusted him. Now for the verse that runs to the blast of ramshorns. *'Et ambulabunt gentes in lumine tuo, et reges in splendore ortus tui.'* How goes that in the Smithy? 'The Gentiles shall come to thy light and Kings to the brightness that springs forth upon thee?' The same in Coverdale, and the Bishops'—eh? We'll keep 'Gentiles,' Ben, for the sake of the indraught of the last syllable. But it might be 'And the Gentiles shall draw.' No! The plainer the better! 'The Gentiles shall come to thy light and Kings to the splendour of——' (Smith's out here! We'll need something that shall lift the trumpet anew.) 'Kings shall—shall—Kings to—' (Listen, Ben, but on your life speak not!) 'Gentiles shall come to thy light and Kings to thy brightness'—No! 'Kings to the brightness that springeth—' Serves not! . . . One trumpet must answer another. And the blast of a trumpet must answer another. And the blast of a trumpet is always *ai-ai*. 'The brightness of'—'*Ortus*' signifies 'rising,' Ben—or what?"

"Ay, or 'birth,' or the East in general."

"Ass! 'Tis the one word that answers to 'light.' 'Kings to the brightness of thy rising.' Look! The thing shines now within and without. God! That so much should lie on a word!" He repeated the verse—"' *And the Gentiles shall come to thy light and Kings to the brightness of thy rising.*'"

He walked to the table and wrote rapidly on the proof margin all three verses as he had spoken them. "If they hold by this," said he, raising his head, "they'll not go far astray. Now for the nineteenth and twentieth verses. On the other sheet, Ben. What? What? Smith says he has held back his rendering till he hath seen mine? Then we'll botch 'em as they stand. Read me first the Latin; next the Coverdale, and last the Bishops'. There's a contagion of sleep in the air." He handed back the proofs, yawned, and took up his walk.

Obedient, Ben began: "'*Non erit tibi amplius Sol ad lucendum per diem, nec splendor Lunae illuminabit te.*' Which Coverdale rendereth, 'The sun shall never go down and thy moon shall have been taken away.' The Bishops' read: 'Thy sun shall never be thy daylight and the light of the moon shall never shine on thee.'"

"Coverdale is better," said Will, and, wrinkling his nose a little, "The Bishops put out their lights clumsily. Have at it, Ben."

Ben pursed his lips and knit his brow. "The two verses are in the same mode, changing a hand's breadth in the second. By so much, therefore, the more difficult."

"Ye see *that*, then?" said the other, staring past him, and muttering as he paced, concerning suns and moons. Presently he took back the proof, chose him another apple and grunted. "Umm-umm! 'Thy Sun shall never go down.' No! Flat as a split viol. '*Non erit tibi amplius Sol*—' That *amplius* must give tongue. Ah! . . . 'Thy Sun shall not— shall not—shall no more be thy light by day' . . . A fair entry. 'Nor'?—No! Not on the heels of 'day.' 'Neither' it must be—'Neither the Moon'—but here's *splendor* and the ramshorns again. (Therefore—*ai-ai!*) 'Neither for brightness shall the Moon.' (Pest! It is the Lord who is taking the Moon's place over Israel. It must be 'thy Moon.') 'Neither for brightness shall thy Moon light—give—make—give light unto thee.' Ah! . . . Listen here! . . . "*The Sun shall no more be thy light by day: neither for brightness shall thy Moon give light unto thee.*' That serves, and more, for the first entry. What next, Ben?"

Ben nodded magisterially as Will neared him, reached out his hand for the proofs, and read: "'*Sed erit tibi Dominus in lucem sempiternam et Deus tuus in gloriam tuam.*' Here is a jewel of Coverdale's that the Bishops have wisely stolen whole. Hear! 'But the Lord Himself shall be thy everlasting light and thy God shall be thy Glory.'" Ben paused. "There's a handsbreadth of splendour for a simple man to gather!"

"Both hands rather. He's swept the strings as divinely as David before Saul," Will assented. "We'll convey it whole, too. . . . What's amiss now, Holofernes?"

For Ben was regarding him with a scholar's cold pit. "Both hands! Will, has thou *ever* troubled to master *any* shape or sort of prosody—the mere names of the measures and pulses of strung words?"

"I beget some such stuff and send it to you to christen. What's your wisdomhood in labour of?"

"Naught. Naught. But not to know the names of the tools of his trade?" Ben half muttered and pronounced some Greek word or other which conveyed nothing to the listener, who replied: "Pardon then for whatever sin it was. I do but know words for my need of 'em, Ben. Hold still awhile!"

He went back to his pacings and mutterings. "'For the Lord Himself shall be thy—or thine?—everlasting light.' Yes, We'll convey that." He repeated it twice. "Nay! Can be bettered. Hark ye, Ben. Here is the Sun going up to over-run and possess all Heaven for evermore. *There*fore (Still, man!) we'll harness the horses of the dawn. Hear their hooves? 'The Lord Himself shall be unto thee thy everlasting light and——" Hold again! After that climbing thunder must be some smooth check—like great wings gliding. *There*fore we'll not have 'shall be thy glory, but *'And* thy God thy glory!' Ay—even as an eagle alighteth! Good—good! Now again, the sun and moon of that twentieth verse, Ben."

Ben read: "'*Non occidet ultra Sol tuus et Luna tua non minuetur: quia erit tibi Dominus in lucem sempiternam, et complebuntur dies luctus tui.*'"

Will snatched the paper and read aloud from the Coverdale version. "'Thy Sun shall never go down and thy Moon shall never be taken away . . .' What a plague's Coverdale doing with his blocking uts and urs, Ben? What's a *minuetur*? . . . I'll have it all anon."

"Minish—make less—appease—abate, as in——"

"So?" . . . Will threw the proofs back. "Then 'wane' should serve. 'Neither shall thy Moon wane' . . . 'Wane' is good, but over-weak for place next to 'moon'" . . . He swore softly. "Isaiah hath abolished both earthly sun and moon. *Exeunt ambo.* Aha! I begin to see! . . . Sol, the man, goes down—downstairs or trap—as needs be. Therefore 'Go down' shall stand. 'Set' would have been better—as a sword sent home in the scabbard—but it jars—it jars. Now Luna must retire herself in some simple fashion . . . Which? Ass that I be! 'Tis common talk in all the plays . . . 'Withdrawn' . . . 'Favour withdrawn' . . . 'Countenance withdrawn.' 'The Queen withdraws herself. For the Lord'— ay, 'the Lord, simple of Himself,' 'shall be thine'—yes, 'thine' here—'everlasting light and' . . How goes the ending, Ben?"

"'*Et complebuntur dies luctus tui,*'" Ben read. "'And thy sorrowful days shall be rewarded thee,' says Coverdale."

"And the Bishops?"

"'And thy sorrowful days shall be ended.'"

"By no means. And Douai?"

"'Thy sorrow shall be ended.'"

"And Geneva?"

"'And the days of thy mourning shall be ended.'"

"The Switzers have it! Lay the tail of Geneva to the head of Coverdale and the last is without flaw." He began to thump Ben on the shoulder. "We have it! I have it all, Boanerges! Blessed be my Demon! Hear! '*The sun shall no more be thy light by day, neither for brightness the moon by night. But the Lord Himself shall be unto thee thy everlasting light and thy God thy glory.*'" He drew a deep breath and went on. "'*Thy sun shall no more go down, neither shall thy moon withdraw herself, for the Lord shall be thine everlasting light and the days of thy mourning shall be ended.*'" The rain of triumphant blows began. "If those other seven devils in London let it stand on this sort, it serves. But God knows what they can *not* turn upsee-dejee!"

Ben wriggled. "Let be!" he protested. "Ye are more moved by this jugglery than if the Globe were burned."

"Thatch—old thatch! And full of fleas! . . . But, Ben, ye should have heard my Ezekiel making mock of fallen Tyrus in his twenty-seventh chapter. Miles sent me the whole, for, he said, some small touches. I took it to the Bank—four o'clock of a summer morn; stretched out in one of our wherries—and watched London, Port and Town, up and down the river, waking all arrayed to heap more upon evident excess. Ay! 'A merchant for the peoples of many isles' . . . 'The ships of Tarshish did sing of thee in thy markets?' Yes! I saw all Tyre before me neighing her pride against lifted heaven . . . But what will they let stand of all mine at long last? Which? I'll never know."

He had set himself neatly and quickly to refolding and cording the packet while he talked. "That's secret enough," he said at the finish.

"He'll lose it by the way." Ben pointed to the sleeper beneath the tree. "He's owl-drunk."

"But not his horse," said Will. He crossed the orchard, roused the man; slid the packet into an holster which he carefully rebuckled; saw him out of the gate, and returned to his chair.

"Who will know we had part in it?" Ben asked.

"God, may be—if He ever lay ear to earth. I've gained and lost enough—lost enough." He lay back and sighed. There was long silence till he spoke half aloud. "And Kit that was my master in the beginning, he died when all the world was young."

"Knifed on a tavern reckoning—not even for a wench!" Ben nodded.

"Ay. But if he'd lived he'd have breathed me! 'Fore God, he'd have breathed me!"

"Was Marlowe, or any man, *ever* thy master, Will?"

"He alone. Very he. I envied Kit. Ye do not know that envy, Ben?"

"Not as touching my own works. When the mob is led to prefer a baser Muse, I have felt the hurt, and paid home. Ye know that—as ye know my doctrine of playwriting."

"Nay—not wholly—tell it at large," said Will, relaxing in his seat, for virtue had gone out of him. He put a few drowsy questions. In three minutes Ben had launched full-flood on the decayed state of the drama, which he was born to correct; on cabals and intrigues against him which he had fought without cease; and on the inveterate muddle-headedness of the mob unless duly scourged into approbation by his magisterial hand.

It was very still in the orchard now that the horse had gone. The heat of the day held though the sun sloped, and the wine had done its work. Presently, Ben's discourse was broken by a snort from the other chair.

"I was listening, Ben! Missed not a word—missed not a word." Will sat up and rubbed his eyes. "Ye held me throughout." His head dropped again before he had done speaking.

Ben looked at him with a chuckle and quoted from one of his own plays:

"'Mine earnest vehement botcher
And deacon also, Will, I cannot dispute with you.'"

He drew out flint, steel and tinder, pipe and tobacco-bag from somewhere round his waist, lit and puffed against the midges till he, too, dozed.

THE DARK LADY OF THE SONNETS

George Bernard Shaw

Fin de siècle 15–1600. Midsummer night on the terrace of the Palace at Whitehall, overlooking the Thames. The Palace clock chimes four quarters and strikes eleven.

A Beefeater on guard. A Cloaked Man approaches.

THE BEEFEATER. Stand. Who goes there? Give the word.

THE MAN. Marry! I cannot. I have clean forgotten it.

THE BEEFEATER. Then cannot you pass here. What is your business? Who are you? Are you a true man?

THE MAN. Far from it, Master Warder. I am not the same man two days together: sometimes Adam, sometimes Benvolio, and anon the Ghost.

THE BEEFEATER [*recoiling*] A ghost! Angels and ministers of grace defend us!

THE MAN. Well said, Master Warder. With your leave I will set that down in writing; for I have a very poor and unhappy brain for remembrance. [*He takes out his tablets and writes*]. Methinks this is a good scene, with you on your lonely watch, and I approaching like a ghost in the moonlight. Stare not so amazedly at me; but mark what I say. I keep tryst here tonight with a dark lady. She promised to bribe the warder. I gave her the wherewithal: four tickets for the Globe Theatre.

THE BEEFEATER. Plague on her! She gave me two only.

THE MAN [*detaching a tablet*] My friend: present this tablet, and you will be welcomed at any time when the plays of Will Shakespear are in hand. Bring your wife. Bring your friends. Bring the whole garrison. There is ever plenty of room.

THE BEEFEATER. I care not for these new-fangled plays. No man can understand a word of them. They are all talk. Will you not give me a pass for the The Spanish Tragedy?

THE MAN. To see The Spanish Tragedy one pays, my friend. Here are the means. [*He gives him a piece of gold*].

THE BEEFEATER [*overwhelmed*] Gold! Oh, sir, you are a better paymaster than your dark lady.

THE MAN. Women are thrifty, my friend.

THE BEEFEATER. Tis so, sir. And you have to consider that the most open handed of us must een cheapen that which we buy every day. This lady has to make a present to a warder nigh every night of her life.

THE MAN [*turning pale*] I'll not believe it.

THE BEEFEATER. Now you, sir, I dare be sworn, do not have an adventure like this twice in the year.

THE MAN. Villain: wouldst tell me that my dark lady hath ever done thus before? that she maketh occasions to meet other men?

THE BEEFEATER. Now the Lord bless your innocence, sir, do you think you are the only pretty man in the world? A merry lady, sir: a warm bit of stuff. Go to: I'll not see her pass a deceit on a gentleman that hath given me the first piece of gold I ever handled.

THE MAN [*intolerantly*] No. All false. All. If thou deny it, thou liest.

THE BEEFEATER. You judge too much by the Court, sir. There, indeed, you may say of frailty that its name is woman.

THE MAN [*pulling out his tablets again*] Prithee say that again: that about frailty: the strain of music.

THE BEEFEATER. What strain of music, sir? I'm no musician, God knows.

THE MAN. There is music in your soul: many of your degree have it very notably. [*Writing*] "Frailty: thy name is woman!" [*Repeating it affectionately*] "Thy name is woman."

THE BEEFEATER. Well, sir, it is but four words. Are you a snapper-up of such unconsidered trifles?

THE MAN [*eagerly*] Snapper-up of—[*he gasps*] Oh! Immortal phrase! [*He writes it down*]. This man is a greater than I.

THE BEEFEATER. You have my lord Pembroke's trick, sir.

THE MAN. Like enough: he is my near friend. But what call you his trick?

THE BEEFEATER. Making sonnets by moonlight. And to the same lady too.

THE MAN. No!

THE BEEFEATER. Last night he stood here on your errand, and in your shoes.

THE MAN. Thou, too, Brutus! And I called him friend!

THE BEEFEATER. Tis ever so, sir.

THE MAN. Tis ever so. Twas ever so. [*He turns away, overcome*]. Two Gentleman of Verona! Judas! Judas!!

THE BEEFEATER. Is he so bad as that, sir?

THE MAN [*recovering his charity and self-possession*] Bad! O no. Human, Master Warder, human. We call one another names when we are offended, as children do. That is all.

THE BEEFEATER. Ay, sir: words, words, words. Mere wind, sir: We fill our bellies with the east wind, sir, as the Scripture hath it. You cannot feed capon so.

THE MAN. A good cadence. By your leave [*He makes a note of it*].

THE BEEFEATER. What manner of thing is a cadence, sir? I have not heard of it.

THE MAN. A thing to rule the world with, friend.

THE BEEFEATER. You speak strangely, sir: no offence. But, an't like you, you are a very civil gentleman, and a poor man feels drawn to you, you being, as twere, willing to share your thought with him.

THE MAN. Tis my trade. But alas! the world for the most part will none of my thoughts.

Lamplight streams from the palace door as it opens from within.

THE BEEFEATER. Here comes your lady, sir. I'll to t'other end of my ward. You may een take your time about your business: I shall not return too suddenly unless my sergeant comes prowling round. Tis a fell sergeant, sir: strict in his arrest. Good een, sir; and good luck! [*He goes*].

THE MAN. "Strict in his arrest"! "Fell sergeant"! [*As if tasting a ripe plum*] O-o-o-h! [*He makes a note of them*].

A Cloaked Lady gropes her way from the palace and wanders along the terrace, walking in her sleep.

THE LADY [*rubbing her hands as if washing them*] Out, damned spot. You will mar all with these cosmetics. God made you one face; and you make yourself another. Think of your grave, woman, not ever of being beautified. All the perfumes of Arabia will not whiten this Tudor hand.

THE MAN. "All the perfumes of Arabia"! "Beautified"! "Beautified"! a poem in a single word. Can this be my Mary? [*To the Lady*] Why do you speak in a strange voice, and utter poetry for the first time? Are you ailing? You walk like the dead. Mary! Mary!

THE LADY [*echoing him*] Mary! Mary! Who would have thought that woman to have had so much blood in her! Is it my fault that my counsellors put deeds of blood on me? Fie! If you were women you would have more wit than to stain the floor so foully. Hold not up her head so: the hair is false. I tell you yet again, Mary's buried: she cannot come out of her grave. I fear her not: these cats that dare jump into thrones though they be fit only for men's laps must be put away. Whats done cannot be undone. Out, I say. Fie! a queen, and freckled!

THE MAN. [*shaking her arm*] Mary, I say: art asleep?

The Lady wakes; starts; and nearly faints. He catches her on his arm.

THE LADY. Where am I? What art thou?

THE MAN. I cry your mercy. I have mistook your person all this while. Methought you were my Mary: my mistress.

THE LADY [*outraged*] Profane fellow: how do you dare?

THE MAN. Be not wroth with me, lady. My mistress is a marvellous proper woman. But she does not speak so well as you. "All the perfumes of Arabia"! That was well said: spoken with good accent and excellent discretion.

THE LADY. Have I been in speech with you here?

THE MAN. Why, yes, fair lady. Have you forgot it?

THE LADY. I have walked in my sleep.

THE MAN. Walk ever in your sleep, fair one; for then your words drop like honey.

THE LADY [*with cold majesty*] Know you to whom you speak, sir, that you dare express yourself so saucily?

THE MAN [*unabashed*] Not I, not care neither. You are some lady of the Court, belike. To me there are but two sorts of women: those with excellent voices, sweet and low, and cackling hens that cannot make me dream. Your voice has all manner of loveliness in it. Grudge me not a short hour of its music.

THE LADY. Sir: you are overbold. Season your admiration for a while with—

THE MAN [*holding up his hand to stop her*] "Season your admiration for a while—"

THE LADY. Fellow: do you dare mimic me to my face?

THE MAN. Tis music. Can you not hear? When a good musician sings a song, do you not sing it and sing it again till you have caught and fixed its perfect melody? "Season your admiration for a while": God! the history of man's heart is in that one word admiration. Admiration! [*Taking up his tablets*] What was it? "Suspend your admiration for a space—"

THE LADY. A very vile jingle of esses. I said "Season your—

THE MAN [*hastily*] Season: ay, season, season, season. Plague on my memory, my wretched memory! I must een write it down. [*He begins to write, but stops, his memory failing him*]. Yet tell me which was the vile jingle? You said very justly: mine own ear caught it even as my false tongue said it.

THE LADY. You said "for a space." I said "for a while."

THE MAN. "For a while" [*he corrects it*]. Good! [*Ardently*] And now be mine neither for a space nor a while, but for ever.

THE LADY. Odds my life! Are you by chance making love to me, knave?

THE MAN. Nay: tis you have have made the love: I but pour it out at your feet. I cannot but love a lass that sets such store by an apt word. Therefore vouchsafe, divine perfection of a woman—no: I have said that before somewhere; and the wordy garment of my love for you must be fire-new—

THE LADY. You talk too much, sir. Let me warn you: I am more accustomed to be listened to than preached at.

THE MAN. The most are like that that do talk well. But though you spake with the tongues of angels, as indeed you do, yet know that I am the king of words—

THE LADY. A king, ha!

THE MAN. No less. We are poor things, we men and women—

THE LADY. Dare you call me woman?

THE MAN. What nobler name can I tender you? How else can I love you? Yet you may well shrink from the name: have I not said we are but poor things? Yet there is a power that can redeem us.

THE LADY. Gramercy for your sermon, sir. I hope I know my duty.

THE MAN. This is no sermon, but the living truth. The power I speak of is the power of immortal poesy. For know that vile as this world is, and worms as we are, you have but to invest all this vileness with a magical garment of words to transfigure us and uplift our souls til earth flowers into a million heavens.

THE LADY. You spoil your heaven with your million. You are extravagant. Observe some measure in your speech.

THE MAN. You speak now as Ben does.

THE LADY. And who, pray, is Ben?

THE MAN. A learned bricklayer who thinks that the sky is at the top of his ladder, and so takes it on him to rebuke me for flying. I tell you there is no word yet coined and no melody yet sung that is extravagant and majestical enough for the glory that lovely words can reveal. It is heresy to deny it: have you not been taught that in the beginning was the Word? that the Word was with God? nay, that the Word was God?

THE LADY. Beware, fellow, how you presume to speak of holy things. The Queen is the head of the Church.

THE MAN. You are the head of my Church when you speak as you did at first. "All the perfumes of Arabia"! Can the Queen speak thus? They say she playeth well upon the virginals. Let her play so to me; and I'll kiss her hands. But until then, you are my Queen; and I'll kiss those lips that have dropt music on my heart. [*He puts his arms about her*].

THE LADY. Unmeasured impudence! On your life, take your hands from me.

The Dark Lady comes stooping along the terrace behind them like a running thrush. When she sees how they are employed, she rises angrily to her full height, and listens jealously.

THE MAN [*unaware of the Dark Lady*] Then cease to make my hands tremble with the streams of life you pour through them. You hold me as the lodestar holds the iron: I cannot but cling to you. We are lost, you and I: nothing can separate us now.

THE DARK LADY. We shall see that, false lying hound, you and your filthy trull. [*With two vigorous cuffs, she knocks the pair asunder, sending the man, who is unlucky enough to receive a righthanded blow, sprawling on the flags*]. Take that, both of you!

THE CLOAKED LADY [*in towering wrath, throwing off her cloak and turning in outraged majesty on her assailant*] High treason!

THE DARK LADY [*recognizing her and falling on her knees in abject terror*] Will: I am lost: I have struck the Queen.

THE MAN [*sitting up as majestically as his ignominious posture allows*] Woman: you have struck WILLIAM SHAKESPEAR!!!!!!

QUEEN ELIZABETH [*stupent*] Marry, come up!!! Struck William Shakespear quotha! And who in the name of all the sluts and jades and light-o'-loves and fly-by-nights that infest this palace of mine, may William Shakespear be?

THE DARK LADY. Madam: he is but a player. Oh, I could have my hand cut off—

QUEEN ELIZABETH. Save you! A likely savior, on my royal word! I had thought this fellow at least an esquire; for I had hoped that even the vilest of my ladies would not have dishonored my Court by wantoning with a baseborn servant.

SHAKESPEAR [*indignantly scrambling to his feet*] Baseborn! I, a Shakespear of Stratford! I, whose mother was an Arden! baseborn! You forget yourself, madam.

ELIZABETH. [*furious*] S'blood! do I so? I will teach you—

THE DARK LADY [*rising from her knees and throwing herself between them*] Will: in God's name anger her no further. It is death. Madam: do not listen to him.

SHAKESPEAR. Not were it een to save your life, Mary, not to mention mine own, will I flatter a monarch who forgets what is due to my family. I deny not that my father was brought down to be a poor bankrupt; but twas his gentle blood that was ever too generous for trade. Never did he disown his debts. Tis true he paid them not; but it is attested truth that he gave bills for them; and twas those bills, in the hands of base hucksters, that were his undoing.

ELIZABETH [*grimly*] The son of your father shall learn his place in the presence of the daughter of Harry the Eighth.

SHAKESPEAR [*swelling with intolerant importance*] Name not that inordinate man in the same breath with Stratford's worthiest alderman. John Shakespear wedded but once: Harry Tudor was married six times. You should blush to utter his name.

THE DARK LADY   { Will: for pity's sake—
crying out together
ELIZABETH   { Insolent dog—

SHAKESPEAR [*cutting them short*] How know you that King Harry was indeed your father?

ELIZABETH.   { Zounds! Now by—[*she stops to grind her teeth with rage*].

THE DARK LADY.   { She will have me whipped through the streets. Oh God! Oh God!

SHAKESPEAR. Learn to know yourself better, madam. I am an honest gentleman of unquestioned parentage, and have already sent in my demand for the coat-of-arms that is lawfully mine. Can you say as much for yourself?

ELIZABETH [*almost beside herself*] Another word; and I begin with mine own hands the work the hangman shall finish.

SHAKESPEAR. You are no true Tudor: this baggage here has as good a right to your royal seat as you. What maintains you on the throne of England? Is it your renownéd wit? your wisdom that sets at nought the craftiest statesmen of the Christian world? No. Tis the mere chance that might have happened to any milkmaid, the caprice of Nature that made you the most wondrous piece of beauty the age hath seen. [*Elizabeth's raised fists, on the point of striking him, fall to her side*]. That is what hath brought all men to your feet, and founded your throne on the impregnable rock of your proud heart, a stony island in a sea of desire. There, madam, is some wholesome blunt honest speaking for you. Now do your worst.

ELIZABETH [*with dignity*] Master Shakespear: it is well for you that I am a merciful prince. I make allowance for your rustic ignorance. But remember that there are things which be true, and yet not seemly to be said (I will not say to a queen; for you will have it that I am none) but to a virgin.

SHAKESPEAR [*bluntly*] It is no fault of mine that you are a virgin, madam, albeit tis my misfortune.

THE DARK LADY [*terrified again*] In mercy, madam, hold no further discourse with him. He hath ever some lewd jest on his tongue. You hear how he useth me! calling me baggage and the like to your Majesty's face.

ELIZABETH. As for you, mistress, I have yet to demand what your business is at this hour in this place, and how you come to be so concerned with a player that you strike blindly at your sovereign in your jealousy of him.

THE DARK LADY. Madam: as I live and hope for salvation—

SHAKESPEAR [*sardonically*] Ha!

THE DARK LADY [*angrily*]—ay, I'm as like to be saved as thou that believest naught save some black magic of words and verses—I say, madam, as I am a living woman I came here to break with him for ever. Oh, madam, if you would know what misery is, listen to this man that is more than man and less at the same time. He will tie you down to anatomize your very soul: he will wring tears of blood from your humiliation; and then he will heal the wound with flatteries that no woman can resist.

SHAKESPEAR. Flatteries! [*Kneeling*] Oh, madam, I put my case at your royal feet. I confess to much. I have a rude tongue: I am unmannerly: I blaspheme against the holiness of anointed royalty; but oh, my royal mistress, *Am* I a flatterer?

ELIZABETH. I absolve you as to that. You are far too plain a dealer to please me. [*He rises gratefully*].

THE DARK LADY. Madam: he is flattering you even as he speaks.

ELIZABETH [*a terrible flash in her eye*] Ha! Is it so?

SHAKESPEAR. Madam: she is jealous; and, heaven help me! not without reason. Oh, you say you are a merciful prince; but that was cruel of you, that hiding of your royal dignity when you found me here. For how can I ever be content with this black-haired, black-eyed, black-avised devil again now that I have looked upon real beauty and real majesty?

THE DARK LADY [*wounded and desperate*] He hath swore to me ten times over that the day shall come in England when black women, for all their foulness, shall be more thought on than fair ones. [*To Shakespear, scolding at him*] Deny it if thou canst. Oh, he is compact of lies and scorns. I am tired of being tossed up to heaven and dragged down to hell at every whim that takes him. I am ashamed to my very soul that I have abased myself to love one that my father would not have deemed fit to hold my stirrup—one that will talk to all the world about me—that will put my love and my shame into his plays and make me blush for myself there—that will write sonnets about me that no man of gentle strain would put his hand to. I am all disordered: I know not what I am saying to your Majesty: I am of all ladies most deject and wretched—

SHAKESPEAR. Ha! At last sorrow hath struck a note of music out of thee. "Of all ladies most deject and wretched." [*He makes a note of it*].

THE DARK LADY. Madam: I implore you to give me leave to go. I am distracted with grief and shame. I—

ELIZABETH. Go. [*The Dark Lady tries to kiss her hand*]. No more. Go. [*The Dark Lady goes, convulsed*]. You have been cruel to that poor fond wretch, Master Shakespear.

SHAKESPEAR. I am not cruel, madam; but you know the fable of Jupiter and Semele. I could not help my lightnings scorching her.

ELIZABETH. You have an overweening conceit of yourself, sir, that displeases your Queen.

SHAKESPEAR. Oh, madam, can I go about with the modest cough of a minor poet, belittling my inspiration and making the mightiest wonder of your reign a thing of nought? I have said that "not marble nor the gilded monuments of princes shall outlive" the words with which I make the world glorious or foolish at my will. Besides, I would have you think me great enough to grant me a boon.

ELIZABETH. I hope it is a boon that may be asked of a virgin Queen without offence, sir. I mistrust your forwardness; and I bid you remember that I do not suffer persons of your degree (if I may say so without offence to your father the alderman) to presume too far.

SHAKESPEAR. Oh, madam, I shall not forget myself again; though by my life, could I make you a serving wench, neither a queen nor a virgin should you be for so much longer as a flash of lightning might take to cross the river to the Bankside. But since you are a queen and will none of me, nor of Philip of Spain, nor of any other mortal man, I must een contain myself as best I may, and ask you only for a boon of State.

ELIZABETH. A boon of State already! You are becoming a courtier like the rest of them. You lack advancement.

SHAKESPEAR. "Lack advancement." By your Majesty's leave: a queenly phrase. [*He is about to write it down*].

ELIZABETH [*striking the tablets from his hand*] Your tablets begin to anger me, sir. I am not here to write your plays for you.

SHAKESPEAR. You are here to inspire them, madam. For this, among the rest, were you ordained. But the boon I crave is that you do endow a great playhouse, or, if I may make bold to coin a scholarly name for it, a National Theatre, for the better instruction and gracing of your Majesty's subjects.

ELIZABETH. Why, sir, are there not theatres enow on the Bankside and in Blackfriars?

SHAKESPEAR. Madam: these are the adventures of needy and desperate men that must, to save themselves from perishing of want, give the sillier sort of people what they best like; and what they best like, God knows, is not their own betterment and instruction, as we well see by the example of the churches, which must needs compel men to frequent them, though they be open to all without charge. Only when there is a matter of a murder, or a plot, or a pretty youth in petticoats, or some naughty tale of wantonness, will your subjects pay the great cost of good players and their finery, with a little profit to boot. To prove this I will tell you that I have written two noble and excellent plays setting forth the advancement of women of high nature and fruitful industry even as your Majesty is: the one a skilful physician, the other a sister devoted to good works. I have also stole from a book of idle wanton tales two of the most damnable foolishnesses in the world, in the one of which a woman goeth in man's attire and maketh impudent love to her swain, who pleaseth the groundlings by overthrowing a wrestler; whilst, in the other, one of the same kidney sheweth her wit by saying endless naughtinesses to a gentleman as lewd as herself. I have writ these to save my friends from penury, yet shewing my scorn for such follies and for them that praise them by calling the one As You Like It, meaning that it is not as I like it, and the other Much Ado About Nothing, as it truly is. And now these two filthy pieces drive their nobler fellows from the stage, where indeed I cannot have my lady physician presented at all, she being too honest a woman for the taste of the town. Wherefore I humbly beg your Majesty to give order that a theatre be endowed out of the public revenue for the playing of those pieces of mine which no merchant will touch, seeing that his gain is so much greater with the worse than with the better. Thereby you shall also encourage other men to undertake the writing of plays who do now despise it and leave it wholly to those whose counsels will work little good to your realm. For this writing of plays is a great matter, forming as it does the minds and affections of men in such sort that whatsoever they see done in show on the stage, they will presently be doing in earnest in the world, which is but a larger stage. Of late, as you know, the Church taught the people by means of plays; but the people flocked only to such as were full of superstitious miracles and bloody martyrdoms; and so the Church, which also was just then brought into straits by the policy of your royal father, did abandon and discountenance the art of playing; and thus it fell into the hands of poor players and greedy merchants that had their pockets to look to and not the greatness of this your kingdom. Therefore now must your Majesty take up that good work that your Church hath abandoned, and restore the art of playing to its former use and dignity.

ELIZABETH. Master Shakespear: I will speak of this matter to the Lord Treasurer.

SHAKESPEAR. Then am I undone, madam; for there was never yet a Lord Treasurer that could find a penny for anything over and above the necessary expenses of your government, save for a war or a salary for his own nephew.

ELIZABETH. Master Shakespear: you speak sooth; yet cannot I in any wise mend it. I dare not offend my unruly Puritans by making so lewd a place as the the playhouse a public charge; and there be a thousand things to be done in this London of mine before your poetry can have its penny from the general purse. I tell thee, Master Will, it will be three hundred years and more before my subjects learn that man cannot live by bread alone, but by every word that cometh from the mouth of those whom God inspires. By that time you and I will be dust beneath the feet of the horses, if indeed there be any horses then, and men be still riding instead of flying. Now it may be that by then your works will be dust also.

SHAKESPEAR. They will stand, madam: fear not for that.

ELIZABETH. It may prove so. But of this I am certain (for I know my countrymen) that until every other country in the Christian world, even to barbarian Muscovy and the hamlets of the boorish Germans, have its playhouse at the public charge, England will never adventure. And she will adventure then only because it is her desire to be ever in the fashion, and to do humbly and dutifully whatso she seeth everybody else doing. In the meantime you must content yourself as best you can by the playing of those two pieces which you give out as the most damnable ever writ, but which your countrymen, I warn you, will swear are the best you have ever done. But this I will say, that if I could speak across the ages to our descendants, I should heartily recommend them to fulfil your wish; for the Scottish minstrel hath well said that he that maketh the songs of a nation is mightier than he that maketh its laws; and the same may well be true of plays and interludes. [*The clock chimes the first quarter. The warder returns on his round*]. And now, sir, we are upon the hour when it better beseems a virgin queen to be abed than to converse alone with the naughtiest of her subjects. Ho there! Who keeps ward on the queen's lodgings tonight?

THE WARDER. I do, an't please your majesty.

ELIZABETH. See that you keep it better in future. You have let pass a most dangerous gallant even to the very door of our royal chamber. Lead him forth; and bring me word when he is safely locked out; for I shall scarce dare disrobe until the palace gates are between us.

SHAKESPEAR [*kissing her hand*] My body goes through the gate into the darkness, madam; but my thoughts follow you.

ELIZABETH. How! to my bed!

SHAKESPEAR. No, madam, to your prayers, in which I beg you to remember my theatre.

ELIZABETH. That is my prayer to posterity. Forget not your own to God; and so goodnight, Master Will.

SHAKESPEAR. Goodnight, great Elizabeth. God save the Queen!

ELIZABETH. Amen.

Exeunt severally: she to her chamber: he, in custody of the warder, to the gate nearest Blackfriars.

LADY MACBETH'S TROUBLE
Letter from Lady Macbeth to Lady Macduff

Maurice Baring

Most Private.

THE PALACE, FORRES
October 10.

My dearest Flora,
 I am sending this letter by Ross, who is starting for Fife to-morrow morning. I wonder if you could possibly come here for a few days. You would bring Jeamie of course. Macbeth is devoted to children. I think we could make you quite comfortable, although of course palaces are never very comfortable, and it's all so different from dear Inverness. And there is the tiresome Court etiquette and the people, especially the Heads of the Clans, who are so touchy, and insist on one's observing every tradition. For instance, the bagpipes begin in the early morning; the pipers walk round

the castle a little after sunrise, and this I find very trying, as you know what a bad sleeper I am. Only two nights ago I nearly fell out of the window walking in my sleep. The doctor, who I must say is a charming man (he was the late King's doctor and King Duncan always used to say he was the only man who really understood his constitution), is giving me mandragora mixed with poppy and syrup; but so far it has not done me any good; but then I always was a wretched sleeper and now I am worse, because—well, I am coming at least to what I really want to say.

I am in very great trouble and I beg you to come here if you can, because you would be the greatest help. You shall have a bedroom facing south, and Jeamie shall be next to you, and my maid can look after you both, and as Macduff is going to England I think it would really be wiser and *safer* for you to come here than to stay all alone in that lonely castle of yours in these troublesome times, when there are so many robbers about and one never knows what may not happen.

I confess I have been very much put about lately. (You quite understand if you come we shall have plenty of opportunities of seeing each other alone in spite of all the tiresome etiquette and ceremonies, and of course you must treat me just the same as before; only in *public* you must just throw in a "Majesty" now and then and curtchey and call me "Ma'am" so as not to shock the people.) I am sorry to say Macbeth is not at all in good case. He is really not at all well, and the fact is he has never got over the terrible tragedy that happened at Inverness. At first I thought it was quite natural he should be upset. Of course very few people know how fond he was of his cousin. King Duncan was his favourite cousin. They had travelled together in England, and they were much more like brothers than cousins, although the King was so much older than he is. I shall never forget the evening when the King arrived after the battle against those horrid Norwegians. I was very nervous as it was, after having gone through all the anxiety of knowing that Macbeth was in danger. Then on the top of that, just after I heard that he was alive and well, the messenger arrived telling me that the King was on his way to Inverness. Of course I had got nothing ready, and Elspeth our housekeeper put on a face as much as to say that we could not possibly manage in the time. However, I said she *must* manage. I knew our cousin wouldn't expect too much, and I spent the whole day making those flat scones he used to be so fond of.

I was already worried then because Macbeth, who is superstitious, said he had met three witches on the way (he said something about it in his letter) and they had apparently been uncivil to him. I thought they were gipsies and that he had not crossed their palm with silver, but when he arrived he was still brooding over this, and was quite *odd* in his way of speaking about it. I didn't think much of this at the time, as I put it down to the strain of what he had gone through, and the reaction which must always be great after such a time; but now it all comes back to me, and now that I think over it in view of what has happened since, I cannot help owning to myself that he was not himself, and if I had not known what a sober man he was, I should almost have thought the 1030 (Hildebrand) whisky had gone to his head—because when he talked of the old women he was quite incoherent: just like a man who has had an hallucination. But I did not think of all this till afterwards, as I put it down to the strain, as I have just told you.

But now! Well, I must go back a little way so as to make everything clear to you. Duncan arrived, and nothing could be more civil than he was. He went out of his way to be nice to everybody and praised the castle, the situation, the view, and even the birds' nests on the walls! (All this, of course, went straight to my heart.) Donalbain and Malcolm were with him. They, I thought at the time, were not at all well brought up. They had not got their father's manners, and they talked in a loud voice and gave themselves airs.

Duncan had supper by himself, and before he went to bed he sent me a most beautiful diamond ring, which I shall always wear. Then we all went to bed. Macbeth was not himself that evening, and he frightened me out of my wits by talking of ghosts and witches and daggers. I did not, however, think anything serious was the matter and I still put it down to the strain and excitement. However, I took the precaution of pouring a drop or two of my sleeping draught into the glass of water which he always drinks before going to bed, so that at least he might have a good night's rest. I suppose I did not give him a strong enough dose. (But one cannot be too careful with drugs, especially mandragora, which is bad for the heart.) At any rate, whether it was that or the awful weather we had that night (nearly all the trees in the park were blown down, and it will never be quite the same again) or whether it was that the hall porter got tipsy (why they choose the one day in the year to drink when one has guests, and it really matters, I never could understand!) and made the most dreadful noise and used really disgraceful language at the front door about five o'clock in the morning, I don't know. At any rate, we were all disturbed long before I had meant that we should be called (breakfast wasn't nearly ready and Elspeth was only just raking out the fires). But, as I say, we were all woken up, and Macduff went to call the King, and came back with the terrible news.

Macbeth turned quite white, and at first my only thought was for him. I thought he was going to have a stroke or a fit. You know he has a very nervous, high-strung constitution, and nothing could be worse for him than a shock like this. I confess that I myself felt as though I wished the earth would open and swallow me up. To think of such a thing happening in our house!

Banquo, too, was as white as a sheet; but the only people who behaved badly (of course this is strictly between ourselves, and I do implore you not to repeat it, as it would really do harm if it got about that I had said this, but you are safe, aren't you, Flora?) were Donalbain and Malcolm. Donalbain said nothing at all, and all Malcolm said when he was told that his father had been murdered was: "Oh! by whom?" I could not understand how he could behave in such a heartless way before so many people; but I must say in fairness that all the Duncans have a very odd way of showing grief.

Of course the first thing I thought was "Who can have done it?" and I suppose in a way it will always remain a mystery. There is no doubt that the chamber grooms actually did the deed; but whether they had any accomplices, whether it was just the act of drunkards (it turned out that the whole household had been drinking that night and not only the hall porter) or whether they were *instigated* by any one else (of course don't quote me as having suggested such a thing) we shall never know. Much as I dislike Malcolm and Donalbain, and shocking as I think their behaviour has been, and not only shocking but, I should not like any one to think that I suspected them of so awful a crime. It is one thing to be bad-mannered, it is another to be a parricide. However, there is no getting over the fact that by their conduct, by their extraordinary behaviour and flight to England, they made people suspect them.

I have only just now come to the real subject of my letter. At first Macbeth bore up pretty well in spite of the blow, the shock, and the extra worry of the coronation following immediately on all this; but no sooner had we settled down at Forres than I soon saw he was far from being himself.

His appetite was bad; he slept badly, and was cross to the servants, making scenes about nothing. When I tried to ask him about his health he lost his temper. At last one day it all came out and I realized that another tragedy was in store for us. Macbeth is suffering from hallucinations; this whole terrible business has unhinged his mind. The doctor always said he was highly strung, and the fact is he has had another attack, or whatever it is, the same as he had after the battle, when he thought he had seen three witches. (I afterwards found out from Banquo, who was with him at the time, that the matter was even worse than I suspected.) He is suffering from a terrible delusion. He thinks (of course you will never breathe this to a soul) that he killed Duncan! You can imagine what I am going through. Fortunately, nobody has noticed it.

Only last night another calamity happened. Banquo had a fall out riding and was killed. That night we had a banquet we could not possibly put off. On purpose I gave strict orders that Macbeth was not to be told of the accident until the banquet was over, but Lennox (who has no more discretion than a parrot) told him, and in the middle of dinner he had another attack, and I had only just time to get every one to go away before he began to rave. As it was, it must have been noticed that he wasn't himself.

I am in a terrible position. I never know when these fits are coming on, and I am afraid of people talking, because if it once gets about, people are so spiteful that somebody is sure to start the rumour that it's true. Imagine our position, then! So I beg you, dear Flora, to keep all this to yourself, and if possible to come here as soon as possible.

I am, your affectionate,

Harriet R.

P.S.—Don't forget to bring Jeamie. It will do Macbeth good to see a child in the house.

SHAKESPEARE'S LIFE

Richard Armour

William Shakespeare, later known as the Beard of Avon, was born in 1564, on April 21, 22, or 23, and all his life kept people guessing. His mother was of gentle birth, but his father, who came of yeoman stock, was born the hard way. The house in which William saw the light is much the same today as it was then, except for the admission charge.[1]

Shakespeare grew up in the little town of Stratford-on-Avon, learning small Latin and less Greek, according to Ben Jonson, probably because he was busy amassing the largest English vocabulary until Noah Webster. For a time he worked for his father, a glover. He was a dreamy lad, which explains the unusual number of four- and six-finger gloves to be found in Stratford antique shops. Subsequently he was bound to a butcher, an awkward situation that kept his nose to the chopping block.

Much of his good taste Shakespeare inherited from his father, who once held the position of ale-taster for the town of Stratford. Young Will made the local team and met the Bidford Sippers in a spirited contest, winning his liter. According to Legend, the chief source of information about Shakespeare's youth, it took him two days to get home from Bidford, which was only a short walk but a long way on hands and knees.

When he was eighteen, Shakespeare met Anne Hathaway, who was eight years older and had begun to give up hope. What he saw in Anne is not known, but he may have admired her thatched roof, as so many have since. At any rate it gave him a good excuse for getting unbound from the butcher. Shakespeare's friends could see no reason for his rushing into marriage, but William and Anne could. Their daughter, Susanna, was born six months later.

Within two years, Shakespeare left for London—alone. Anne had given birth to twins, and there was no telling what she would do next. Moreover, he was accused of poaching something in a deer park, and it wasn't an egg.

Between 1585 and 1592 little is known of Shakespeare. These are the Lost Years, a period fraught with mystery and much more frustrating than the Lost Weekend. It may be that Shakespeare went into a deep sleep, like Rip Van Winkle, or wandered around in a daze, unaware of the execution of Mary Queen of Scots, the defeat of the Spanish Armada, and the introduction of the Irish potato. One authority, believing that Shakespeare must have been doing something of which he was ashamed, conjectures that he was a schoolteacher. This gave him access to the library, where he surreptitiously copied the plots of old plays for future use.

Some credence is given to the theory that Shakespeare during this period was holding horses outside a theater.[2] After eight years, he became one of the most experienced horse-holders in London. It was at this time that he began to write, holding the reins in one hand and a pen in the other.

His earliest history plays were on the reins of Henry VI and Richard III, internal evidence being the famous line in the latter play, "A horse! A horse! My kingdom for a horse!" a cry which Shakespeare must often have heard from departing theatergoers on rainy nights.

Shakespeare was very versatile. Besides being a successful playwright, he was an actor and part owner of the theater. Once when they were short of scenery he painted himself green and played a tree. When not otherwise occupied, he sold tickets at the box office and souvenir programs in the aisles. This gave rise to the theory that there were six William Shakespeares, additional evidence being the six signatures in the British Museum, each spelled a different way. But there were actually only two: the Man and the Myth.

Several times Shakespeare acted in plays at the court of Queen Elizabeth, but the Queen was too busy watching Essex to notice. When King James came to the throne, Shakespeare was made one of the King's Men, a company of actors who had the right to protection from the King after a bad performance. Shakespeare never really excelled as an actor, but since he wrote the lines it was easy for him to learn them.

This was Merrie England, and Shakespeare had a gay time in London, his wife and children being in Stratford. He was often seen at the Mermaid Tavern, imbibing with Ben Jonson and the sons of Ben, who were sent to watch out for their father and carry him home. But his favorite pub was the Temple Bar. "Drink to me only with thine eyes," Ben was fond of saying, but Shakespeare knew he didn't mean a word of it. "O rare Ben Jonson," he would remark, clinking canikins with his friend and quaffing the good English ale.[3]

In his last years, having had his fun, Shakespeare returned to Stratford and lived with his wife. When he died, he bequeathed her his second-best bed, the one with the broken springs and the crack in the headboard. Who got his number one bed is a dark secret.

Over Shakespeare's grave is an inscription that says: "Curst be he that moves my bones." So far as is known, the bones have never been moved in all these years. It is possible, of course, that this book may make Shakespeare turn over in his grave, but in that case he will have moved them himself.

NOTES

[1]Actually Shakespeare was not born in the Birthplace but in the Museum, a fact which he found embarrassing and kept secret from all but his closest friends.

[2]Unless they were held, they went inside to watch the play.

[3]No matter how rare Ben was to start with, by the end of the evening he was usually well done, in fact completely stewed.

FROM BEOWULF
TO VIRGINIA WOOLF

Robert Manson Myers

William Shakespeare was the greatest dramatist the world has yet to produce. He came of a very respectable family and was, through no fault of his own, born poor but honest on a hot and paltry day in 1564, presumably on his birthday, near Suffix, England, while his parents were travailing abroad. In extreme youth, having already marred Anne Hatchaway, the Merry Widow, he settled at Windsor with his eight merry wives, where he remained until 1611, when he removed to Stratford-on-Auburn, more commonly known as the Deserted Village. Shakespeare never made much money, and he is remembered today chiefly for his plays, most of which have, unfortunately, been dramatized. In early manhood he wrote *Love's Labour's Lust,* to be followed shortly by *As You Lack It* (a high comedy, featuring the villainous Skylark), and *Anatomy and Coleoptera* (a comedy of errors):

Age cannot wither nor costume stale
Her indefinite virginity.

In later manhood he wrote *Othello* (the first domestic
tragedy), *King Lear* (the last domestic tragedy), and *Hamlet*
(a tragedy of errors). Shakespeare betrayed women
brilliantly: he created female characters with a stroke of his
pen, and it is impossible to find a Hamlet among them.
Although he was a dramatist of vast proportions, he
sometimes also wrote poetry: *The Rape of Lucretius* was
inspired by the works of Seneca, a Roman prefix under
Emperor Trojan. Shakespeare wrote almost exclusively in
blank verse (unrhymed ironic pentameter); and his plays
often present a fool—sometimes Shakespeare himself.

THE NAMING OF THE GLOBE

Caryl Brahms and S. J. Simon

In the manager's office over on the Bankside, Burbage and his playwright were in conference. They were sharing Hal Eight's throne, using Juliet's coffin as a table, and the canopy from *Hal Four* had been hurriedly moved into position to keep a sudden shower off their heads.

They were collaborating.

"Tell you what," said Burbage, "we'll call it the court."

"C-A-U-T," wrote Shakespeare. "No," he said firmly, "that is no name for a theater."

"It is very appropriate," said Burbage, hurt, "for it is maintained by favor and surrounded by conspiracies."

"And nobody goes there if they can avoid it," said Shakespeare. "No—we will not call our theater this."

"Burbage thought again.

"Let us," he suggested, "call it the Bankside."

"B-Y-N-K-S-Y-D," wrote Shakespeare. He shook his head. "It is too local. Master Burbage, I have a better idea. Let us call our theater the London."

"L-U-N-D-U-N," wrote Burbage. "Master Will, I have a better idea still. Let us call it England. Merrie England," he added.

Shakespeare did not attempt to spell this out. "Old-fashioned," he said. "Stinks of *Hal Eight*. The theater," he explained, "must be living, universal, and should speak for all men at all times."

They concentrated.

"The English Channel," muttered Burbage. "The Indian Ocean." He shook his head. "The Seven Seas." He frowned.

"Tell you what," said Shakespeare, inspired. "We'll call it the GLOBE."

"G-O-L-B," wrote Burbage. He nodded, well satisfied.

The Collaboration had arrived at a successful conclusion.

MR. K*A*P*L*A*N AND
SHAKESPEARE

Leonard Q. Ross
(Leo Rosten)

It was Miss Higby's idea in the first place. She had
suggested to Mr. Parkhill that the students came to her class
unaware of the *finer* side of English, of its beauty and, as
she put it, "the glorious heritage of our literature." She
suggested that perhaps poetry might be worked into the
exercises of Mr. Parkhill's class. The beginners' grade had,
after all, been subjected to almost a year of English and
might be presumed to have achieved some linguistic
sophistication. Poetry would make the students conscious of
precise enunciation; it would make them read with greater
care and an ear for sounds. Miss Higby, who had once
begun a master's thesis on Coventry Patmore, *loved* poetry.
And, it should be said in all justice, she argued her cause
with considerable logic. Poetry *would* be excellent for the
enunciation of the students, thought Mr. Parkhill.

161

So it was that when he faced the class the following Tuesday night, Mr. Parkhill had a volume of Shakespeare on his desk, and an eager, almost an expectant, look in his eye. The love that Miss Higby bore for poetry in general was as nothing compared to the love that Mr. Parkhill bore for Shakespeare in particular. To Mr. Parkhill, poetry meant Shakespeare. Many years ago he had played Polonius in his senior class play.

"Tonight, class," said Mr. Parkhill, "I am going to try an experiment."

The class looked up dutifully. They had come to regard Mr. Parkhill's pedagogical innovations as part of the natural order.

"I am going to introduce you to poetry—great poetry. You see—" Mr. Parkhill delivered a modest lecture on the beauty of poetry, its expression of the loftier thoughts of men, its economy of statement. He hoped it would be a relief from spelling and composition exercises to use poetry as the subject matter of the regular Recitation and Speech period. "I shall write a passage on the board and read it for you. Then, for Recitation and Speech, you will give short addresses, using the passage as the general topic, telling us what it has brought to your minds, what thoughts and ideas."

The class seemed quite pleased by the announcement. Miss Mitnick blushed happily. (This blush was different from most of Miss Mitnick's blushes; there was aspiration and idealism in it.) Mr. Norman Bloom sighed with a business-like air: you could tell that for him poetry was merely another assignment, like a speech on "What I Like to Eat Best" or a composition on "A Day at a Picnic." Mrs. Moskowitz, to whom any public performance was unpleasant, tried to look enthusiastic, without much success. And Mr. Hyman Kaplan, the heroic smile on his face as indelibly as ever, looked at Mr. Parkhill with admiration and

whispered to himself: "Poyetry! Now is poyetry! My! Mus'
be progriss ve makink awreddy!"

"The passage will be from Shakespeare," Mr. Parkhill
announced, opening the volume.

An excited buzz ran through the class as the magic of that
name fell upon them.

"Imachine!" murmured Mr. Kaplan. "Jakesbeer!"
"*Shakes*peare, Mr. Kaplan!"

Mr. Parkhill took a piece of chalk and, with care and
evident love, wrote the following passage on the board in
large, clear letters:

> Tomorrow, and tomorrow, and tomorrow
> Creeps in this petty pace from day to day,
> To the last syllable of recorded time;
> And all our yesterdays have lighted fools
> The way to dusty death. Out, out, brief candle!
> Life's but a walking shadow, a poor player
> That struts and frets his hour upon the stage,
> And then is heard no more; it is a tale
> Told by an idiot, full of sound and fury,
> Signifying nothing.

A reverent hush filled the classroom, as eyes gazed with
wonder on this passage from the Bard. Mr. Parkhill was
pleased at this.

"I shall read the passage first," he said. "Listen carefully
to my enunciation—and—er—let Shakespeare's thoughts
sink into your minds."

Mr. Parkhill read: "'Tomorrow, and tomorrow, and
tomorrow . . .'" Mr. Parkhill read very well and this night,
as if some special fire burned in him, he read with rare
eloquence. "Out, out, brief candle!" In Miss Mitnick's eyes
there was inspiration and wonder. "Life's but a walking
shadow . . ." Mrs. Moskowitz sat with a heavy frown,

indicating cerebration. "It is a tale told by an idiot . . ." Mr. Kaplan's smile had taken on something luminous; but his eyes were closed: it was not clear whether Mr. Kaplan had surrendered to the spell of the Immortal Bard or to that of Morpheus.

"I shall—er—read the passage again," said Mr. Parkhill, clearing his throat vociferously until he saw Mr. Kaplan's eyes open. "'Tomorrow, and tomorrow, and tomorrow....'"

When Mr. Parkhill had read the passage for the second time, he said: "That should be quite clear now. Are there any questions?"

There were a few questions. Mr. Scymzak wanted to know whether "frets" was "a little kind excitement." Miss Schneiderman asked about "struts." Mr. Kaplan wasn't sure about "cripps." Mr. Parkhill explained the words carefully, with several illustrative uses of each word. "No more questions? Well, I shall allow a few minutes for you all to— er—think over the meaning of the passage. Then we shall begin Recitation and Speech."

Mr. Kaplan promptly closed his eyes again, his smile beatific. The students sank into that revery miscalled thought, searching their souls for the symbols evoked by Shakespeare's immortal words.

"Miss Caravello, will you begin?" asked Mr. Parkhill at last.

Miss Caravello went to the front of the room. "Da poem isa gooda," she said slowly. "Itsa have—"

"It *has*."

"It hasa beautiful wordsa. Itsa lak Dante, Italian poet—"

"Ha!" cried Mr. Kaplan scornfully. "Shaksbeer you metchink mit Tante? *Shakesbeer*? Mein Gott!"

It was obvious that Mr. Kaplan had identified himself with Shakespeare and would tolerate no disparagement of his *alter ego*.

"Miss Caravello is merely expressing her own ideas," said Mr. Parkhill pacifically. (Actually, he felt completely sympathetic to Mr. Kaplan's point of view.)

"Hau Kay," agreed Mr. Kaplan, with a generous wave of the hand. "But to me is no comparink a high-cless man like Shaksbeer mit a Tante, dat's all."

Miss Caravello, her poise shattered, said a few more words and sat down.

Mrs. Yampolsky's contribution was brief. "This is full deep meanings," she said, her eyes on the floor. "Is hard for a person not so good in English to unnistand. But I like."

"'*Like!*'" cried Mr. Kaplan with a fine impatience. "'*Like?*' Batter *love*, Yampolsky. Mit Shaksbeer mus' be *love!*"

Mr. Parkhill had to suggest that Mr. Kaplan control his aesthetic passions. He did understand how Mr. Kaplan felt, however, and sensed a new bond between them. Mrs. Yampolsky staggered through several more nervous comments and retired.

Mr. Bloom was next. He gave a long declamation, ending: "So is passimistic ideas in the poem, and I am optimist. Life should be happy—so we should remember this is only a poem. Maybe is Shakespeare too passimistic."

"You wronk, Bloom!" cried Mr. Kaplan with prompt indignation. "Shaksbeer is passimist because is de *life* passimist also!"

Mr. Parkhill, impressed by this philosophical stroke, realized that Mr. Kaplan, afire with the glory of the Swan of Avon, could not be suppressed. Mr. Kaplan was the kind of man who brooked no criticism of his gods. The only solution was to call on Mr. Kaplan for his recitation at once. Mr. Parkhill was, indeed, curious about what fresh thoughts Mr. Kaplan would utter after his passionate defenses of the Bard. When Mr. Parkhill had corrected certain parts of Mr.

Bloom's speech, emphasizing Mr. Bloom's failure to use the indefinite article, he said: "Mr. Kaplan, will *you* speak next?"

Mr. Kaplan's face broke into a glow; his smile was like a rainbow. "Soitinly," he said, walking to the front of the room. Never had he seemed so dignified, so eager, so conscious of a great destiny.

"Er—Mr. Kaplan," added Mr. Parkhill, suddenly aware of the possibilities which the situation (Kaplan on Shakespeare) involved: "Speak *carefully*."

"*Spacially* careful vil I be," Mr. Kaplan reassured him. He cleared his throat, adjusted his tie, and began: "Ladies an' gantleman, you hoid all kinds minninks abot dis piece poyetry, an'—"

"*Poe*try."

"—abot dis piece *po*etry. But to me is a difference minnink altogadder. Ve mus' tink abot Julius Scissor an' how *he* falt!"

Mr. Parkhill moved nervously, puzzled.

"In dese exact voids is Julius Scissor sayink—"

"Er—Mr. Kaplan," said Mr. Parkhill once he grasped the full import of Mr. Kaplan's error. "The passage is from 'Macbeth.'"

Mr. Kaplan looked at Mr. Parkhill with injured surprise. "*Not* fromm 'Julius Scissor'?" There was pain in his voice.

"No. And it's—er—'Julius *Cae*sar.'"

Mr. Kaplan waited until the last echo of the name had permeated his soul. "Podden me, Mr. Pockheel. Isn't '*see*zor' vat you cottink somting up mit?"

"That," said Mr. Parkhill quickly, "is 'scissor.' You have used 'Caesar' for 'scissor' and 'scissor' for 'Caesar.'"

Mr. Kaplan nodded, marvelling at his own virtuosity.

"But go on with your speech, please." Mr. Parkhill, to tell the truth, felt a little guilty that he had not announced at

the very beginning that the passage was from "Macbeth."
"Tell us *why* you thought the lines were from 'Julius
Caesar.'"

"Vell," said Mr. Kaplan to the class, his smile assuming
its normal serenity. "I was positif, becawss I can *see* de
whole ting." He paused, debating how to explain this cryptic
remark. Then his eyes filled with a strange enchantment. "I
see de whole scinn. It's in a tant, on de night bafore dey
makink Julius de Kink fromm Rome. So he is axcited an'
ken't slip. He is layink in bad, tinking: 'Tomorrow an'
tomorrow an' tomorrow. How slow dey movink! Almost
cripps! Soch a pity de pace!'"

Before Mr. Parkhill could explain that "petty pace" did
not mean "Soch a pity de pace!" Mr. Kaplan had soared on.

"De days go slow, fromm day to day, like leetle
tsyllables on phonograph racords fromm time."

Anxiety and bewilderment invaded Mr. Parkhill's eyes.

"'An' vat abot yestidday?' tinks Julius Scissor. Ha! 'All
our yestiddays are only makink a good light for fools to die
in de dost!'"

"'Dusty death' doesn't mean—" There was no
interrupting Mr. Kaplan.

"An' Julius Scissor is so tired, an' he vants to fallink
aslip. So he hollers, mit fillink, "Go ot! Go ot! Short
candle!' So it goes ot."

Mr. Kaplan's voice dropped to a whisper. "But he ken't
slip. Now is bodderink him de idea fromm life. 'Vat is de
life altogadder?' tinks Julius Scissor. An' he gives enswer,
de pot I like de bast. 'Life is like a bum actor, strottink an'
hollerink arond de stage for only vun hour bafore he's
kicked ot. Life is a tale told by idjots, dat's all, full of fonny
sonds an' phooey!'"

Mr. Parkhill could be silent no longer. "'Full of sound and fury!'" he cried desperately. But inspiration, like an irresistible force, swept Mr. Kaplan on.

"'Life is monkey business! It don' minn a ting. It signifies nottink!' An' den Julius Scissor closes his ice fest—" Mr. Kaplan demonstrated the Consul's exact ocular process in closing his "ice"—"—an' falls dad!"

The class was hushed as Mr. Kaplan stopped. In the silence, a tribute to the fertility of Mr. Kaplan's imagination and the power of his oratory, Mr. Kaplan went to his seat. But just before he sat down, as if adding a postscript, he sighed: "Dat was mine idea. But ufcawss is all wronk, becawss Mr. Pockheel said de voids ain't abot Julius Scissor altogadder. It's all abot an Irishman by de name Macbat."

Then Mr. Kaplan sat down.

It was some time before Mr. Parkhill could bring himself to criticize Mr. Kaplan's pronunciation, enunciation, diction, grammar, idiom, and sentence structure. For Mr. Parkhill discovered that he could not easily return to the world of reality. He was still trying to tear himself away from that tent outside Rome, where "Julius Scissor," cursed with insomnia, had thought of time and life—and philosophized himself to a strange and sudden death.

Mr. Parkhill was distinctly annoyed with Miss Higby.

THE MACBETH MURDER MYSTERY

James Thurber

"It was a stupid mistake to make," said the American woman I had met at my hotel in the English lake country, "but it was on the counter with the other Penguin books—the little sixpenny ones, you know, with the paper covers—and I supposed of course it was a detective story. All the others were detective stories. I'd read all the others, so I bought this one without really looking at it carefully. You can imagine how mad I was when I found it was Shakespeare." I murmured something sympathetically. "I don't see why the Penguin-books people had to get out Shakespeare plays in the same size and everything as the detective stories," went on my companion. "I think they have different-colored jackets," I said. "Well, I didn't notice that," she said. "Anyway, I got real comfy in bed that night and all ready to read a good mystery story and here I had 'The Tragedy of Macbeth'—a book for high-school students. Like 'Ivanhoe,'" "Or 'Lorna Doone,'" I said. "Exactly," said the

American lady. "And I was just crazy for a good Agatha
Christie, or something. Hercule Poirot is my favorite
detective." "Is he the rabbity one?" I asked. "Oh, no," said
my crime-fiction expert. "He's the Belgian one. You're
thinking of Mr. Pinkerton, the one that helps Inspector Bull.
He's good, too."

Over her second cup of tea my companion began to tell
the plot of a detective story that had fooled her completely—
it seems it was the old family doctor all the time. But I cut in
on her. "Tell me," I said. "Did you read 'Macbeth'?" "I *had*
to read it," she said. "There wasn't a scrap of anything else
to read in the whole room." "Did you like it?" I asked. "No,
I did not," she said decisively. "In the first place, I don't
think for a moment that Macbeth did it." I looked at her
blankly. "Did what?" I asked. "I don't think for a moment
that he killed the King," she said. "I don't think the Macbeth
woman was mixed up in it, either. You suspect them the
most, of course, but those are the ones that are never
guilty—or shouldn't be, anyway." "I'm afraid," I began,
"that I—" "But don't you see?" said the American lady. "It
would spoil everything if you could figure out right away
who did it. Shakespeare was too smart for that. I've read
that people never *have* figured out 'Hamlet,' so it isn't likely
Shakespeare would have made 'Macbeth' as simple as it
seems." I thought this over while I filled my pipe. "Who do
you suspect?" I asked, suddenly. "Macduff," she said,
promptly. "Good God!" I whispered, softly.

"Oh Macduff did it, all right," said the murder specialist.
"Hercule Poirot would have got him easily." "How did you
figure it out?" I demanded. "Well," she said, "I didn't right
away. At first I suspected Banquo. And then, of course, he
was the second person killed. That was good right in there,
that part. The person you suspect of the first murder should
always be the second victim." "Is that so?" I murmured.

"Oh, yes," said my informant. "They have to keep surprising you. Well, after the second murder I didn't know *who* the killer was for a while." "How about Malcolm and Donalbain, the King's sons?" I asked. "As I remember it, they fled right after the first murder. That looks suspicious." "Too suspicious," said the American lady. "Much too suspicious. When they flee, they're never guilty. You can count on that." "I believe," I said, "I'll have a brandy," and I summoned the waiter. My companion leaned toward me, her eyes bright, her teacup quivering. "Do you know who discovered Duncan's body?" she demanded. I said I was sorry, but I had forgotten. "Macduff discovers it," she said, slipping into the historical present. "Then he comes running downstairs and shouts, 'Confusion has broke open the the Lord's anointed temple' and 'Sacrilegious murder has made his masterpiece' and on and on like that." The good lady tapped me on the knee. "All that stuff was rehearsed," she said. "You wouldn't say a lot of stuff like that, offhand, would you—if you had found a body?" She fixed me with a glittering eye. "I—" I began. "You're right!" she said. "You wouldn't! Unless you had practiced it in advance. 'My God, there's a body in here!' is what an innocent man would say." She sat back with a confident glare.

I thought for a while. "But what do you make of the Third Murderer?" I asked. "You know, the Third Murderer has puzzled 'Macbeth' scholars for three hundred years." "That's because they never thought of Macduff," said the American lady. "It was Macduff, I'm certain. You couldn't have one of the victims murdered by two ordinary thugs— the murderer always has to be somebody important." "But what about the banquet scene?" I asked, after a moment. "How do you account for Macbeth's guilty actions there, when Banquo's ghost came in and sat in his chair?" The lady leaned forward and tapped me on the knee again. "There wasn't any ghost," she said. "A big, strong man like that doesn't go around seeing ghosts—especially in a brightly lighted banquet hall with dozens of people around. Macbeth was *shielding somebody*!" "Who was he shielding?" I asked. "Mrs. Macbeth, of course," she said. "He thought she did it and he was going to take the rap himself. The husband always does that when the wife is suspected." "But what," I demanded, "about the sleepwalking scene, then?" "The same thing, only the other way around," said my companion. "That time *she* was shielding *him*. She wasn't asleep at all. Do you remember where it says, 'Enter Lady Macbeth with a taper'?" "Yes," I said. "Well, people who walk in their sleep *never carry lights*!" said my fellow-traveler. "They have a second sight. Did you ever hear of a sleepwalker carrying a light?" "No," I said, "I never did." "Well, then, she wasn't asleep. She was acting guilty to shield Macbeth." "I think," I said, "I'll have another brandy," and I called the waiter. When he brought it, I drank it rapidly and rose to go. "I believe," I said, "that you have got hold of something. Would you lend me that 'Macbeth'? I'd like to look it over tonight. I don't feel, somehow, as if I'd ever really read it." "I'll get it for you," she said. "But you'll find that I am right."

I read the play over carefully that night, and the next morning, after breakfast, I sought out the American woman. She was on the putting green, and I came up behind her silently and took her arm. She gave an exclamation. "Could I see you alone?" I asked in a low voice. She nodded cautiously and followed me to a secluded spot. "You've found out something?" she breathed. "I've found out," I said, triumphantly, "the name of the murderer!" "You mean it wasn't Macduff?" she said. "Macduff is as innocent of those murders," I said, "as Macbeth and the Macbeth woman." I opened the copy of the play, which I had with me, and turned to Act II, Scene 2. "Here," I said, "you will see where Lady Macbeth says, 'I laid their daggers ready. He could not miss 'em. Had he not resembled my father as he slept, I had done it.' Do you see?" "No," said the American woman, bluntly, "I don't." "But it's simple!" I exclaimed. "I wonder I didn't see it years ago. The reason Duncan resembled Lady Macbeth's father as he slept is that *it actually was her father!*" "Good God!" breathed my companion, softly. "Lady Macbeth's father killed the King," I said, "and, hearing someone coming, thrust the body under the bed and crawled into the bed himself." "But," said the lady, "you can't have a murderer who only appears in the story once. You can't have that." "I know that," I said, and I turned to Act II, Scene 4. "It says here, 'Enter Ross with an old Man.' Now, that old man is never identified and it is my contention he was old Mr. Macbeth, whose ambition it was to make his daughter Queen. There you have your motive." "But even then," cried the American lady, "he's still a minor character!" "Not," I said, gleefully, "when you realize that he was also *one of the weird sisters in disguise!*" "You mean one of the three witches?" "Precisely," I said. "Listen to this speech of the old man's. 'On Tuesday last, a falcon towering in her pride of place, was by a mousing owl hawk'd and kill'd.' Who does that sound like?" "It sounds like the way the three witches talk," said my companion, reluctantly. "Precisely!" I said again. "Well," said the American woman, "maybe you're right, but—" "I'm sure I am," I said. "And do you know what I'm going to do now?" "No," she said. "What?" "Buy a copy of 'Hamlet,'" I said, "and solve *that!*" My companion's eye brightened. "Then," she said, "you don't think Hamlet did it?" "I am," I said, "absolutely positive he didn't." "But who," she demanded, "do you suspect?" I looked at her cryptically. "Everybody," I said, and disappeared into a small grove of trees as silently as I had come.

RING OUT, WILD BELLS

Wolcott Gibbs

When I finally got around to seeing Max Reinhardt's cinema version of "A Midsummer-Night's Dream," and saw a child called Mickey Rooney playing Puck, I remembered suddenly that long ago I had taken the same part.

Our production was given on the open-air stage at the Riverdale Country School, shortly before the war. The scenery was only the natural scenery of that surburban dell, and the cast was exclusively male, ranging in age from eleven to perhaps seventeen. While we had thus preserved the pure, Elizabethan note of the original, it must be admitted that our version had its drawbacks. The costumes were probably the worst things we had to bear, and even Penrod, tragically arrayed as Launcelot in his sister's stockings and his father's drawers, might have been embarrassed for us. Like Penrod, we were costumed by our parents, and like the Schofields, they seemed on the whole a little weak historically. Half of the ladies were inclined to favor the

Elizabethan, and they had constructed rather bunchy ruffs and farthingales for their offspring; others, who had read as far as the stage directions and learned that the action took place in an Athenian wood, had produced something vaguely Athenian, usually beginning with a sheet. Only the fairies had a certain uniformity. For some reason their parents had all decided on cheesecloth, with here and there a little ill-advised trimming with tinsel.

My own costume was mysterious, but spectacular. As nearly as I have ever been able to figure things out, my mother found her inspiration for it in a Maxfield Parrish picture of a court jester. Beginning at the top, there was a cap with three stuffed horns; then, for the main part, a pair of tights that covered me to my wrists and ankles; and finally slippers with stuffed toes that curled up at the ends. The whole thing was made out of silk in alternate green and red stripes, and (unquestionably my poor mother's most demented stroke) it was covered from head to foot with a thousand tiny bells. Because all our costumes were obviously perishable, we never wore them in rehearsal, and naturally nobody knew that I was invested with these peculiar sound effects until I made my entrance at the beginning of the second act.

Our director was a man who had strong opinions about how Shakespeare should be played, and Puck was one of his favorite characters. It was his theory that Puck, being "the incarnation of mischief," never ought to be still a minute, so I had been coached to bound onto the stage, and once there to dance up and down, cocking my head and waving my arms.

"I want you to be a little whirlwind," this man said.

Even as I prepared to bound onto the stage, I had my own misgivings about those dangerously abundant gestures, and their probable effect on my bells. It was too late, however, to invent another technique for playing Puck, even if there had been room for anything but horror in my mind. I bounded onto the stage.

The effect, in its way, must have been superb. With every leap I rang like a thousand children's sleighs, my melodies foretelling God knows what worlds of merriment to the enchanted spectators. It was even worse when I came to the middle of the stage and went into my gestures. The other ringing had been loud but sporadic. This was persistent, varying only slightly in volume and pitch with the vehemence of my gestures. To a blind man, it must have sounded as though I had recklessly decided to accompany myself on a xylophone. A maturer actor would probably have made up his mind that an emergency existed, and abandoned his gestures as impracticable under the circumstances. I was thirteen, and incapable of innovations. I had been told by responsible authorities that gestures went with this part, and I continued to make them. I also continued to ring—a silvery music, festive and horrible.

If the bells were hard on my nerves, they were even worse for the rest of the cast, who were totally unprepared for my new interpretation. Puck's first remark is addressed to one of the fairies, and it is mercifully brief.

I said, "How now, spirit! Whither wander you?"

This unhappy child, already embarrassed by a public appearance in cheesecloth and tinsel, was also burdened with an opening speech of sixteen lines in verse. He began bravely:

> "Over hill, over dale,
>   Through brush, through brier,
> Over park, over pale,
>   Through flood, through fire . . ."

At the word "fire," my instructions were to bring my hands up from the ground in a long, wavery sweep, intended to represent fire. The bells pealed. To my startled ears, it sounded more as if they exploded. The fairy stopped in his lines and looked at me sharply. The jingling, however, had diminished; it was no more than as if a faint wind stirred my bells, and he went on:

> "I do wander everywhere,
> Swifter than the moone's sphere ..."

Here again I had another cue, for a sort of swoop and dip indicating the swiftness of the moone's sphere. Again the bells rang out, and again the performance stopped in its tracks. The fairy was clearly troubled by these interruptions. He had, however, a child's strange acceptance of the inscrutable, and was even able to regard my bells as a last-minute adult addition to the program, nerve-racking but not to be questioned. I'm sure it was only this that got him through that first speech.

My turn, when it came, was even worse. By this time the audience had succumbed to a helpless gaiety. Every time my bells rang, laughter swept the spectators, and this mounted and mingled with the bells until everything else was practically inaudible. I began my speech, another long one, and full of incomprehensible references to Titania's changeling.

"Louder!" said somebody in the wings. "You'll have to talk louder."

It was the director, and he seemed to be in a dangerous state.

"And for heaven's sake, stop that jingling!" he said.

I talked louder, and I tried to stop the jingling, but it was no use. By the time I got to the end of my speech, I was shouting and so was the audience. It appeared that I had very little control over the bells, which continued to jingle in spite of my passionate efforts to keep them quiet.

All this had a very bad effect on the fairy, who by this time had many symptoms of a complete nervous collapse. However, he began his next speech:

> "Either I mistake your shape and making quite,
> Or else you are that shrewd and knavish sprite
> Called Robin Goodfellow: are you not he
> That . . ."

At this point I forgot that the rules had been changed and I was supposed to leave out the gestures. There was a furious jingling, and the fairy gulped.

> "Are you not he that, that . . ."

He looked miserably at the wings, and the director supplied the next line, but the tumult was too much for him. The unhappy child simply shook his head.

"Say anything!" shouted the director desperately. "Anything at all!"

The fairy only shut his eyes and shuddered.

"All right!" shouted the director. "All right, Puck. *You* begin *your* next speech."

By some miracle, I actually did remember my next lines, and had opened my mouth to begin on them when suddenly the fairy spoke. His voice was a high, thin monotone, and there seemed to be madness in it, but it was perfectly clear.

"Fourscore and seven years ago," he began, "our fathers brought forth on this continent a new nation, conceived . . ."

He said it right through to the end, and it was certainly the most successful speech ever made on that stage, and probably one of the most successful speeches ever made on any stage. I don't remember, if I ever knew, how the rest of us ever picked up the dull, normal thread of the play after that extraordinary performance, but we must have, because I know it went on. I only remember that in the next intermission the director cut off my bells with his penknife, and after that things quieted down and got dull.

THE SKINHEAD HAMLET

Richard Curtis

*Shakespeare's Play translated into modern English.
"our hope was to achieve something like the effect of the
New English Bible." Eds.*

ACT I—Scene 1
*The Battlements of Elsinore Castle.
(enter Hamlet, followed by Ghost.)*

Ghost: Oi! Mush!
Hamlet: Yer?
Ghost: I was fucked!

        (exit Ghost.)

Hamlet: O fuck.

        (exit Hamlet.)

Scene 2. The Throneroom.
(enter King Claudius, Gertrude, Hamlet and Court.)

Claudius: Oi! You, Hamlet: give over!
Hamlet: Fuck off, won't you?
              exit Claudius, Gertrude, Court.)
Hamlet: (alone.) They could have fucking waited.
                    (enter Horatio.)
Horatio: Oi! Whatcha cock!
Hamlet: Weeeey!

                    (*exeunt.*)

              Scene 3. Ophelia's Bedroom.
              (*enter Ophelia and Laertes.*)

Laertes: I'm fucking off now. Watch Hamlet doesn't slip
       you one while I'm gone.
Ophelia: I'll be fucked if he does.
                    (*exeunt.*)

              Scene 4. The Battlements.
         (*enter Horatio, Hamlet and Ghost.*)

Ghost: Oi! Mush, get on with it!
Hamlet: Who did it then?
Ghost: That wanker Claudius. He poured fucking poison in
       my fucking ear!
Hamlet: Fuck me!

                    (*exeunt.*)

         ACT II. Scene 1. A corridor in the castle.
         (*enter Hamlet reading. Enter Polonius.*)

Poloni: Oi! You!
Hamlet: Fuck off, grandad!
         (*exit Polon. Enter Rosencrantz and Guildenstern.*)
Ros & Gu.: Oi! Oi! Mucca!

Hamlet: Fuck off, the pair of you!
        (*exit Ros and Guild.*)
Hamlet: (alone) To fuck or be fucked.
        (*enter Ophelia.*)
Ophelia: My lord!
Hamlet: Fuck off to a nunnery!
        (*they exit in different directions.*)

ACT III. Scene 1. Throne Room.
(*enter Players and all Court.*)

1 Player: Full thirty time hath Phoebus cart . . .
Claudius: I'll be fucked if I watch any more of this crap.
        (*exeunt.*)

Scene 2. Gertrude's Bedchamber.
(*enter Hamlet, to Gertrude.*)

Hamlet: Oi! Slag!
Gertrude: Watch your fucking mouth, kid!
Polon.: (*from behind the curtain*) Too right.
Hamlet: Who the fuck was that?
        (*he stabs Polonius through the arras.*)
Polon.: Fuck!
Hamlet: Fuck! I thought it was that other wanker.
        (*exeunt.*)

ACT 4. Scene 1. Court Room.

Claudius: Fuck off to England then!
Hamlet: Delighted, mush.

Scene 2. Throneroom.
(*Ophelia, Gertrude and Claudius.*)

Ophelia: Here, cop a whack of this.
  (*she hands Gertrude some rosemary and exits.*)
Claudius: She's fucking round the twist, in't she?
Gertrude: (*looking out the window.*) There is a willow
  grows aslant the brook.
Claudius: Get on with it, slag.
Gertrude: Ophelia's gone and fucking drowned!
Claudius: Fuck! Laertes isn't half going to be browned off.
  (*exeunt.*)

Scene 3. A Corridor.

Laertes: (*alone.*) I'm going to fucking do this lot.
  (*enter Claudius*)
Claudius: I didn't fucking do it, mate. It was that wanker
  Hamlet.
Laertes: Well, fuck him.

ACT 5. Scene 1. Hamlet's Bedchamber.
  (*Hamlet and Horatio seated.*)

Hamlet: I got this feeling I'm going to cop it, Horatio, and
  you know, I couldn't give a flying fuck.
  (*exeunt.*)

Scene 2. Large Hall.
  (*enter Hamlet, Laertes, Court, Gertrude, Claudius.*)

Laertes: Oi, wanker: let's get on with it!
Hamlet: Delighted, fuckface.
  (*they fight and both are poisoned by the poisoned sword.*)
Laertes: Fuck!
Hamlet: Fuck!
  (*the Queen drinks.*)

Gertrude: Fucking odd wine!

Claudius: You drunk the wrong fucking cup, you stupid cow!

Hamlet: (*pouring the poison down Claudius' throat.*) Well, fuck you!

Claudius: I'm fair and squarely fucked.

Laertes: Oi, mush: no hard feelings, he?

Hamlet: Yer.

(*Laertes dies.*)

Hamlet: Oi! Horatio!

Horatio: Yer?

Hamlet: I'm fucked. The rest is fucking silence.

(*Hamlet dies.*)

Horatio: Fuck: that was no ordinary wanker, you know.

(*enter Fortinbras.*)

Fortin.: What the fuck's going on here?

Horatio: A fucking mess, that's for sure.

Fortin.: No kidding. I see Hamlet's fucked.

Horatio: Yer.

Fortin.: Fucking shame: fucking good bloke.

Horatio: Too fucking right.

Fortin.: Fuck this for a lark then. Let's piss off.

(*exeunt with alarums.*)

THE IMMORTAL BARD

Isaac Asimov

"Oh, yes," said Dr. Phineas Welch, "I can bring back the spirits of the illustrious dead."

He was a little drunk, or maybe he wouldn't have said it. Of course, it was perfectly all right to get a little drunk at the annual Christmas party.

Scott Robertson, the school's young English instructor, adjusted his glasses and looked to right and left to see if they were overheard. "Really, Dr. Welch."

"I mean it. And not just the spirits. I bring back the bodies, too."

"I wouldn't have said it were possible," said Robertson primly.

"Why not? A simple matter of temporal transference."

"You mean time travel? But that's quite—uh—unusual."

"Not if you know how."

"Well, how, Dr. Welch?"

"Think I'm going to tell you?" asked the physicist gravely. He looked vaguely about for another drink and didn't find any. He said, "I brought quite a few back. Archimedes, Newton, Galileo. Poor fellows."

"Didn't they like it here? I should think they'd have been fascinated by our modern science," said Robertson. He was beginning to enjoy the conversation.

"Oh, they were. They were. Especially Archimedes. I thought he'd go mad with joy at first after I explained a little of it in some Greek I'd boned up on, but no—no—"

"What was wrong?"

"Just a different culture. They couldn't get used to our way of life. They got terribly lonely and frightened. I had to send them back."

"That's too bad."

"Yes. Great minds, but not flexible minds. Not universal. So I tried Shakespeare."

"*What?*" yelled Robertson. This was getting closer to home.

"Don't yell, my boy," said Welch. "It's bad manners."

"Did you say you brought back Shakespeare?"

"I did. I needed someone with a universal mind; someone who knew people well enough to be able to live with them centuries way from his own time. Shakespeare was the man. I've got his signature. As a memento, you know."

"On you?" asked Robertson, eyes bugging.

"Right here." Welch fumbled in one vest pocket after another. "Ah, here it is."

A little piece of pasteboard was passed to the instructor. On one side it said: "L. Klein & Sons, Wholesale Hardware." On the other side, in straggly script, was written, "Willm Shakesper."

A wild surmise filled Robertson. "What did he look like?"

"Not like his pictures. Bald and an ugly mustache. He spoke in a thick brogue. Of course, I did my best to please him with our times. I told him we thought highly of his plays and still put them on the boards. In fact, I said we thought they were the greatest pieces of literature in the English language, maybe in any language."

"Good. Good," said Robertson breathlessly.

"I said people had written volumes of commentaries on his plays. Naturally he wanted to see one and I got one for him from the library."

"And?"

"Oh, he was fascinated. Of course, he had trouble with the current idioms and references to events since 1600, but I helped out. Poor fellow. I don't think he ever expected such treatment. He kept saying, 'God ha' mercy! What cannot be racked from words in five centuries? One could wring, methinks, a flood from a damp clout!'"

"He wouldn't say that."

"Why not? He wrote his plays as quickly as he could. He said he had to on account of the deadlines. He wrote *Hamlet* in less than six months. The plot was an old one. He just polished it up."

"That's all they do to a telescope mirror. Just polish it up," said the English instructor indignantly.

The physicist disregarded him. He made out an untouched cocktail on the bar some feet away and sidled toward it. "I told the immortal bard that we even gave college courses in Shakespeare."

"I give one."

"I know. I enrolled him in your evening extension course. I never saw a man so eager to find out what posterity thought of him as poor Bill was. He worked hard at it."

"You enrolled William Shakespeare in my course?" mumbled Robertson. Even as an alcoholic fantasy, the thought staggered him. And *was* it an alcoholic fantasy? He was beginning to recall a bald man with a queer way of talking. . . .

"Not under his real name, of course," said Dr. Welch. "Never mind what he went under. It was a mistake, that's all. A big mistake. Poor fellow." He had the cocktail now and shook his head at it.

"Why was it a mistake? What happened?"

"I had to send him back to 1600," roared Welch indignantly. "How much humiliation do you think a man can stand?"

"What humiliation are you talking about?"

Dr. Welch tossed off the cocktail. "Why, you poor simpleton, you *flunked* him."

SHAKESPEARE THE PHYSICIST

Banesh Hoffmann

I have not often known Sherlock Holmes to jest. But Holmes and I have both become more mellow, and a growing humour and warm sentiment have enriched our latter years.

As we lingered over breakfast at our annual reunion last Christmas, Holmes, who had been unusually silent, idly fingered some books that he had brought to the table. I glanced curiously at the titles. "Well, Holmes," I said, "what is the case to be this time?"

"I am afraid, my dear Watson, that I have no case to tell you this Christmas," he replied. And then, seeing my disappointment, he hastened to add, "But I have something just as good."

"Literary research has always attracted me," he continued with a mischievous twinkle in his eye. "For in no other field does the art of detection find such free rein. I am embodying the results of my recent investigations in a little monograph

that may have important influence on Shakespearean
scholarship. My discoveries suggest the need for a complete
revaluation of Shakespeare's works. For they imply that his
writings conceal, beneath a cloak of poetry and drama,
unparalleled feats of clairvoyance and prognostication."

I was about to protest, but he stilled me with a gesture.

"The first hints of this startling possibility came no more
than a few decades ago. With the advent of wireless
broadcasting, men began to look for hidden meanings in *The
Tempest*, their attention roused by the prophetic name of the
character Ariel."

"But the spelling is wrong," I burst out.

Holmes frowned at the interruption. "Surely you are
aware that Shakespeare, like other Elizabethans, was
notoriously careless in his spelling. . . . Scholars pointed out
that the play was full of magical happenings that often bore
uncanny resemblance to the modern miracles of wireless; so
much so that Ariel might well be the personification of
wireless itself. They persisted in their researches and soon
came upon a striking passage that they felt could not be
easily laughed away.

"I have here Caliban's speech in Act 2, Scene 3 of *The
Tempest*, telling of the magic performed by Ariel and
Prospero. Permit me to read a little of it:

> *Be not afeared; the isle is full of noises,*
> *Sounds and sweet airs, that give delight and hurt not.*
> *Sometimes a thousand twangling instruments*
> *Will hum about mine ears, and sometimes voices. . . .*

"Why," I cried, "this is extraordinary. It is wireless to
the life. A modern could hardly have described it more aptly.
Even the announcer is there."

Holmes chuckled and went on: "My own recent discoveries, which are concerned mainly with the *Sonnets*, bring the strongest possible support to the thesis of the early researchers. Listen, for instance, to the beginning of *Sonnet 12*:

> *When I do count the clock that tells the time*
> *And see the brave day sunk in hideous night. . . .*

"It reads like poesy pure and simple. But I shall now point out to you unmistakable indications that these lines refer to Einstein's theory of relativity."

"My dear Holmes!"

"You think it unlikely? Did not Einstein arrive at his theory by rejecting the notion of absolute time? Did he not reason in terms of the behavior of clocks moving relative to one another? Did he not, in the words of Shakespeare, *count the clock that tells the time*? In one small line Shakespeare has packed the essence of the theory of relativity."

"Surely it is rather farfetched," I murmured dubiously.

"Oh, yes. One line alone can easily be dismissed as a coincidence. But once we realize that the sonnet refers to the theory of relativity the significance of the second line is immediately clear. How was Einstein's theory tested? Was it not during a total eclipse of the sun, with *the brave day in hideous night*? If this is still a coincidence it is by now an enormous one."

"Holmes," I laughed. "I am convinced."

"My dear Watson, I have hardly begun to present the evidence. Shakespeare's 64th sonnet describes the present atomic situation so aptly that every line of it can be understood as a message for today."

He paced nervously up and down as I read the following:

> *When I have seen by Time's fell hand defaced*
> *The rich proud cost of outworn buried age;*
> *When sometime lofty towers I see downrazed*
> *And brass eternal slave to mortal rage;*
> *When I have seen the hungry ocean gain*
> *Advantage on the kingdom of the shore,*
> *And the firm soil win of the watery main,*
> *Increasing store with loss and loss with store;*
> *When I have seen such interchange of state,*
> *Or state itself confounded to decay;*
> *Ruin hath taught me thus to ruminate,*
> *That Time will come and take my love away.*
> *This thought is as a death, which cannot choose*
> *But weep to have that which it fears to lose.*

I was puzzled. "There is nothing here about the atomic bomb. Are you sure this is the one you meant?"

"Certainly. How does it begin?"

> *When I have seen by Time's fell hand defaced*

"Just so. In view of the 12th sonnet we have just discussed, we may take *Time* to refer to relativity and thus to Einstein's famous equation $E=mc^2$. For the correct continuity we must skip to the third line: *When sometime lofty towers we see down—razed*. These are the steel towers that supported the atomic bomb in the first bomb test in New Mexico in July of 1945. Truly the *lofty towers* were *down—razed* by $E=mc^2$. It is, of course, hardly necessary to add that the word *sometimes* means that the test occurred in the summer time."

"Hardly necessary at all," I murmured.

"How does the second line go?"

> *The rich proud cost of outworn buried age*

"Ah, yes. This seems obscure at first. But only if we do Shakespeare the injustice of assuming that he did not foresee the modern method of estimating the age of the rocks. This is done by examining the by-products of their decaying radioactive constituents. If Shakespeare knew of this, was it not the height of poesy for him to speak of uranium deposits as *outworn buried age*? The *rich proud cost* needs no further explanation. We are all taxpayers. Kindly read the fourth line."

I read the cryptic words: *And brass eternal slave to mortal rage.*

"Now, Watson, this is something recherché. Observe closely. The key to its meaning is the pair of words *slave to*. This is an ingenious contraction, formed by combining two v's into one. Separate them out and we have the phrase Slav veto, which refers unmistakably to the behaviour of the Russian delegation to the United Nations. The *Slav veto* is here characterized as *brass eternal* and we are told that it engenders in us *mortal rage*."

"I am delighted to find Shakespeare on our side in the cold war," I remarked.

"The next three lines are to be taken together," said Holmes.

> *When I have seen the hungry ocean gain*
> *Advantage on the kingdom of the shore,*
> *And the firm soil win of the watery main*

"This has to do with the Bikini bomb tests, which sent a shower of radioactive water over the island of Bikini, a *kingdom of the shore* from which the king and his subjects had previously been removed. The island was not obliterated. The *firm soil* won over the *watery main*. You see how admirably it all fits? What is the next line?"

Increasing store with loss and loss with store

"That is an easy one. As you see, it foretells the *increasing store* of atomic bombs in stockpiles, the words *loss and loss* being, of course, an oblique reference to Los Alamos, where the bombs were first designed. I see you are enjoying my little monograph."

"Indeed I am. It is positively delightful. I have never known you more brilliantly entertaining. But how do you explain the next line?"

When I have seen such interchange of state

"Ah. This is one for the specialists. It is a highly technical reference, showing how thoroughly Shakespeare understood the nature of modern atomic theory. Atomic physicists will recognize *interchange of state* as the purest quantum theory. And as if this were not enough indication, Shakespeare goes on, in the following line, to talk of *state itself confounded to decay*. This clearly refers to the radioactive decay of an atom, which is associated with a change in the quantum state of the nucleus.

"The next line, *Ruin hath taught me thus to ruminate*, with its ominous opening word, tells subtly of the hydrogen bomb. For some reason Shakespeare decided to make the reference obscure. Perhaps he was unable to decide whether a hydrogren bomb could be made to work or not. Be that as it may, the reference is definitely there, if one will but look for it. Observe the innocent word *hath*. If we write it *H at H*, it succinctly expresses the idea of hurling hydrogen nuclei at hydrogen nuclei, which is one way of causing nuclear fusion. To explode an H-bomb one needs a fission bomb, and Shakespeare suggests this, too. Split the word *ruminate*—*rumina* is an almost perfect anagram of uranium,

and *te* gives the first and last letters of two hundred and
thirty-five, the explosive isotope.

"The next line is a melancholy one:

That Time will come and take my love away.

"Here *love* refers to the American monopoly of the
atomic bomb, which was indeed our love. And time has
already come and taken it away. *This thought is as a death,*
Shakespeare goes on to say. Could one put it more
tragically? And what of the final line: *But weep to have that*
which it fears to lose? Does it not sum up the awful dilemma
of modern man? We do not want the atomic bomb. We
should all sleep far more soundly did it not exist. Certainly
we weep to have that which we fear to lose."

There was a moment of silence. Holmes reached for
another book. "Since we began with *The Tempest*, it is
fitting that *The Tempest* have the last word. If you still
entertain doubts as to Shakespeare's prophetic powers,
ponder this dire prediction of atomic destruction. It is from
Act 4, Scene 1:

The cloud-capp'd towers, the gorgeous palaces,
The solemn temples, the great globe itself,
Yea, all which it inherit, shall dissolve
And, like this insubstantial pageant faded,
Leave not a rack behind.

I could not suppress a sigh.

"Cheer up, Watson. Perhaps men will be wise and it will
not come to that. Perhaps, after all, Shakespeare is not the
prophet I have made him out to be. I trust you have enjoyed
my Christmas fable despite its sombre ending. Indeed, I

perceive that you have, for you have let your breakfast get cold. Have some warm eggs, Watson."

"Thank you, Holmes. But no more bacon."

pete the parrot and shakespeare

Don Marquis

i got acquainted with
a parrot named pete recently
who is an interesting bird
pete says he used
to belong to the fellow
that ran the mermaid tavern
in london then i said
you must have known
shakespeare know him said pete
poor mutt i knew him well
he called me pete and i called him
bill but why do you say poor mutt
well said pete bill was a
disappointed man and was always
boring his friends about what
he might have been and done
if he only had a fair break

two or three pints of sack
and sherris and the tears
would trickle down into his
beard and his beard would get
soppy and wilt his collar

i remember one night when
bill and ben jonson and
frankie beaumont
were sopping it up

here i am ben says bill
nothing but a lousy playwright
and with anything like luck
in the breaks i might have been
a fairly decent sonnet writer
i might have been a poet
if i had kept away from the theatre

yes says ben i ve often
thought of that bill
but one consolation is
you are making pretty good money
out of the theatre

money money says bill what the hell
is money what i want is to be
a poet not a business man
these damned cheap shows
i turn out to keep the
theatre running break my heart
slap stick comedies and
blood and thunder tragedies
and melodramas say i wonder

if that boy heard you order
another bottle frankie
the only compensation is that i get
a chance now and then
to stick in a little poetry
when nobody is looking
but hells bells that isn t
what i want to do
i want to write sonnets and
songs and spenserian stanzas
and i might have done it too
if i hadn t got
into this frightful show game
business business business
grind grind grind
what a life for a man
that might have been a poet

well says frankie beaumont
why don t you cut it bill
i can t says bill
i need the money i ve got
a family to support down in
the country well says frankie
anyhow you write pretty good
plays bill any mutt can write
plays for this london public
says bill if he puts enough
murder in them what they want
is kings talking like kings
never had sense enough to talk
and stabbings and stranglings
and fat men making love
and clowns basting each

other with clubs and cheap puns
and off color allusions to all
the smut of the day oh i know
what the low brows want
and i give it to them

well says ben johnson
don t blubber into the drink
brace up like a man
and quit the rotten business
i can t i can t says bill
i ve been at it too long i ve got to
the place now where i can t
write anything else
but this cheap stuff
i m ashamed to look an honest
young sonneteer in the face
i live a hell of a life i do
the manager hands me some mouldy old
manuscript and says
bill here s a plot for you
this is the third of the month
by the tenth i want a good
script out of this that we
can start rehearsals on
not too big a cast
and not too much of your
damned poetry either
you know your old familiar line of hokum
they eat up that falstaff stuff
of yours ring him in again
and give them a good ghost
or two and remember we gotta
have something dick burbage can get

his teeth into and be sure
and stick in a speech
somewhere the queen will take
for a personal compliment and if
you get in a line or two somewhere
about the honest english yeoman
it s always good stuff
and it s a pretty good stunt
bill to have the heavy villain
a moor or a dago or a jew
or something like that and say
i want another
comic welshman in this
but i don t need to tell
you bill you know this game
just some of your ordinary
hokum and maybe you could
kill a little kid or two a prince
or something they like
a little pathos along with
the dirt now you better see burbage
tonight and see what he wants
in that part oh says bill
to think i am
debasing my talents with junk
like that oh god what i wanted
was to be a poet
and write sonnet serials
like a gentleman should

well says i pete
bill s plays are highly
esteemed to this day
is that so says pete

poor mutt little he would
care what poor bill wanted
was to be a poet

archy

From *ULYSSES*

James Joyce

—We want to hear more, John Eglinton decided with Mr Best's approval. We begin to be interested in Mrs S. Till now we had thought of her, if at all, as a patient Griselda, a Penelope stayathome.

—Antisthenes, pupil of Gorgias, Stephen said, took the palm of beauty from Kyrios Menelaus' brooddam, Argive Helen, the wooden mare of Troy in whom a score of heroes slept, and handed it to poor Penelope. Twenty years he lived in London and, during part of that time, he drew a salary equal to that of the lord chancellor of Ireland. His life was rich. His art, more than the art of feudalism, as Walt Whitman called it, is the art of surfeit. Hot herringpies, green mugs of sack, honeysauces, sugar of roses, marchpane, gooseberried pigeons, ringocandies. Sir Walter Raleigh, when they arrested him, had half a million francs on his back including a pair of fancy stays. The gombeen woman Eliza Tudor had underlinen enough to vie with her of

Sheba. Twenty years he dallied there between conjugal love and its chaste delights and scortatory love and its foul pleasures. You know Manningham's story of the burgher's wife who bade Dick Burbage to her bed after she had seen him in *Richard III* and how Shakespeare, overhearing, without more ado about nothing, took the cow by the horns and, when Burbage came knocking at the gate, answered from the capon's blankets: *William the conqueror came before Richard III.* And the gay lakin, Mistress Fitten, mount and cry O, and his dainty birdsnies, Lady Penelope Rich, a clean quality woman is suited for a player, and the punks of the bankside, a penny a time.

Cours-la-Reine. *Encore vingt sous. Nous ferons de petites cochonneries. Minette? Tu veux?*

—The height of fine society. And sir William Davenant of Oxford's mother with her cup of canary for every cockcanary.

Buck Mulligan, his pious eyes upturned, prayed:

—Blessed Margaret Mary Anycock!

—And Harry of six wives' daughter and other lady friends from neighbour seats, as Lawn Tennyson, gentleman poet, sings. But all those twenty years what do you suppose poor Penelope in Stratford was doing behind the diamond panes?

Do and do. Thing done. In a rosery of Fetter Lane of Gerard, herbalist, he walks, greyedauburn. An azured harebell like her veins. Lids of Juno's eyes, violets. He walks. One life is all. One body. Do. But do. Afar, in a reek of lust and squalor, hands are laid on whiteness.

Buck Mulligan rapped John Eglinton's desk sharply.

—Whom do you suspect? he challenged.

—Say that he is the spurned lover in the sonnets. Once spurned twice spurned. But the court wanton spurned him for a lord, his dearmylove.

—Love that dare not speak its name.

—As an Englishman, you mean, John sturdy Eglinton put in, he loved a lord.

Old wall where sudden lizards flash. At Charenton I watched them.

—It seems so, Stephen said, when he wants to do for him, and for all other and singular uneared wombs, the holy office an ostler does for the stallion. Maybe, like Socrates, he had a midwife to mother as he had a shrew to wife. But she, the giglot wanton, did not break a bedvow. Two deeds are rank in that ghost's mind: a broken vow and the dullbrained yokel on whom her favour has declined, deceased husband's brother, Sweet Ann I take it, was hot in the blood. Once a wooer twice a wooer.

Stephen turned boldly in his chair.

—The burden of proof is with you not with me, he said, frowning. If you deny that in the fifth scene of *Hamlet* he has branded her with infamy, tell my why there is no mention of her during the thirtyfour years between the day she married him and the day she buried him. All those women saw their men down and under: Mary, her goodman John, Ann, her poor dear Willun, when he went and died on her, raging that he was the first to go, Joan, her four brothers, Judith, her husband and all her sons, Susan, her husband too, while Susan's daughter, Elizabeth, to use granddaddy's words, wed her second, having killed her first.

O yes, mention there is. In the years when he was living richly in royal London to pay a debt she had to borrow forty shillings from her father's shepherd. Explain you then. Explain the swansong too wherein he has commended her to posterity.

He faced their silence.

To whom thus Eglinton:

You mean the will.
That has been explained, I believe, by jurists.
She was entitled to her widow's dower
At common law. His legal knowledge was great
Our judges tell us.
                              Him Satan fleers,
Mocker:
              And therefore he left out her name
From the first draft but he did not leave out
The presents for his granddaughter, for his
daughters,
              For his sister, for his old cronies in Stratford
And in London. And therefore when he was urged,
As I believe, to name her
He left her his
Secondbest
Bed.
                                        Punkt

Leftherhis
Secondbest
Bestabed
Secabest
Leftabed.

Woa!

—Pretty countryfolk had few chattels then, John Eglinton observed, as they have still if our peasant plays are true to type.

—He was a rich countrygentleman, Stephen said, with a coat of arms and landed estate at Stratford and a house in Ireland yard, a capitalist shareholder, a bill promoter, a tithe-farmer. Why did he not leave her his best bed if he wished her to snore away the rest of her nights in peace?

—It is clear that there were two beds, a best and a secondbest, Mr Secondbest Best said finely.

—*Separatio a mensa et a thalamo*, bettered Buck Mulligan and was smiled on.

—Antiquity mentions famous beds, Second Eglinton puckered, bedsmiling. Let me think.

—Antiquity mentions that Stagyrite schoolurchin and bald heathen sage, Stephen said, who when dying in exile frees and endows his slaves, pays tribute to his elders, wills to be laid in earth near the bones of his dead wife and bids his friends be kind to an old mistress (don't forget Nell Gwynn Herpyllis) and let her live in his villa.

—Do you mean he died so? Mr Best asked with slight concern. I mean . . .

—He died dead drunk, Buck Mulligan capped. A quart of ale is a dish for a king. O, I must tell you what Dowden said!

—What? asked Besteglinton.

William Shakespeare and company, limited. The people's William. For terms apply: E. Dowden, Highfield house . . .

—Lovely! Buck Mulligan suspired amorously. I asked him what he thought of the charge of pederasty brought against the bard. He lifted his hands and said: *All we can say is that life ran very high in those days.* Lovely!

Catamite.

—The sense of beauty leads us astray, said beautifulinsadness Best to ugling Eglinton.

Steadfast John replied severe:

—The doctor can tell us what those words mean. You cannot eat your cake and have it.

Sayest thou so? Will they wrest from us, from me the palm of beauty?

—And the sense of property, Stephen said. He drew Shylock out of his own long pocket. The son of a maltjobber and moneylender he was himself a cornjobber and moneylender with ten tods of corns hoarded in the famine riots. His borrowers are no doubt those divers of worship mentioned by Chettle Falstaff who reported his uprightness of dealing. He sued a fellowplayer for the price of a few bags of malt and exacted his pound of flesh in interest for every money lent. How else could Aubrey's ostler and callboy get rich quick? All events brought grist to his mill. Shylock chimes with the jewbaiting that followed the hanging and quartering of the queen's leech Lopez, his jew's heart being plucked forth while the sheeny was yet alive: *Hamlet* and *Macbeth* with the coming to the throne of a Scotch philosophaster with a turn for witchroasting. The lost armada is his jeer in *Love's Labour Lost*. His pageants, the histories, sail fullbellied on a tide of Mafeking enthusiasm. Warwickshire jesuits are tried and we have a porter's theory of equivocation. The *Sea Venture* comes home from Bermudas and the play Renan admired is written with Patsy Caliban, our American cousin. The sugared sonnets follow Sidney's. As for fay Elizabeth, otherwise carroty Bess, the gross virgin who inspired *The Merry Wives of Windsor,* let some meinherr from Almany grope his life long for deep-hid meanings in the depth of the buckbasket.

I think you're getting on very nicely. Just mix up a mixture of theologicophilological. *Mingo, minxi, mictum, mingere.*

—Prove that he was a jew, John Eglinton dared, expectantly. Your dean of studies holds he was a holy Roman.

Sufflaminandus sum.

—He was made in Germany, Stephen replied, as the champion French polisher of Italian scandals.

—A myriadminded man, Mr Best reminded. Coleridge called him myriadminded.

Amplius. In societate humana hoc est maxime necessarium ut sit amicitia inter multos.

—Saint Thomas, Stephen began . . .

—*Ora pro nobis,* Monk Mulligan groaned, sinking to a chair.

There he keened a wailing rune.

—*Pogue mahone! Acushla machree!* It's destroyed we are from this day! It's destroyed we are surely!

All smiled their smiles.

—Saint Thomas, Stephen, smiling, said, whose gorbellied works I enjoy reading in the original, writing of incest from a standpoint different from that of the new Viennese school Mr Magee spoke of, likens it in his wise and curious way to an avarice of the emotions. He means that the love so given to one near in blood is covetously withheld from some stranger who, it may be, hungers for it. Jews, whom christians tax with avarice, are of all races the most given to inter-marriage. Accusations are made in anger. The christian laws which built up the hoards of the jews (for whom, as for the lollards, storm was shelter) bound their affections too with hoops of steel. Whether these be sins or virtues old Nobodaddy will tell us at doomsday leet. But a man who holds so tightly to what he calls his rights over what he calls his debts will hold tightly also to what he calls his rights over her whom he calls his wife. No sir smile neighbour shall covet his ox or his wife or his manservant or his maidservant or his jackass.

—Or his jennyass, Buck Mulligan antiphoned.

—Gentle Will is being roughly handled, gentle Mr Best said gently.

—Which Will? gagged sweetly Buck Mulligan. We are getting mixed.

—The will to live, John Eglinton philosophised, for poor Ann, Will's widow, is the will to die.

—*Requiescat!* Stephen prayed.

What of all the will to do?
It has vanished long ago . . .

—She lies laid out in stark stiffness in that secondbest bed, the mobled queen, even though you prove that a bed in those days was as rare as a motor car is now and that its carvings were the wonder of seven parishes. In old age she takes up with gospellers (one stayed at New Place and drank a quart of sack the town paid for but in which bed he slept it skills not to ask) and heard she had a soul. She read or had read to her his chapbooks preferring them to the *Merry Wives* and, loosing her nightly waters on the jordan, she thought over *Hooks and Eyes for Believers' Breeches* and *The Most Spiritual Snuffbox to Make the Most Devout Souls Sneeze.* Venus had twisted her lips in prayer. Agenbite of inwit: remorse of conscience. It is an age of exhausted whoredom groping for its god.

—History shows that to be true, *inquit Eglintonus Chronologos.* The ages succeed one another. But we have it on high authority that a man's worst enemies shall be those of his own house and family. I feel that Russell is right. What do we care for his wife and father? I should say that only family poets have family lives. Falstaff was not a family man. I feel that the fat knight is his supreme creation.

Lean, he lay back. Shy, deny thy kindred, the unco guid. Shy supping with the godless, he sneaks the cup. A sire in Ultonian Antrim bade it him. Visits him here on quarter days. Mr Magee, sir, there's a gentleman to see you. Me? Says he's your father, sir. Give me my Wordsworth. Enter Magee Mor Matthew, a rugged rough rugheaded kern, in strossers with a buttoned codpiece, his nether stocks bemired with clauber of ten forests, a wand of wilding in his hand.

Your own? He knows your old fellow. The widower. Hurrying to her squalid deathlair from gay Paris on the quayside I touched his hand. The voice, new warmth, speaking. Dr Bob Kenny is attending her. The eyes that wish me well. But do not know me.

—A father, Stephen said, battling against hopelessness, is a necessary evil. He wrote the play in the months that followed his father's death. If you hold that he, a greying man with two marriageable daughters, with thirtyfive years of life, *nel mezzo del cammin di nostra vita*, with fifty of experience, is the beardless undergraduate from Wittenberg then you must hold that his seventyyear old mother is the lustful queen. No. The corpse of John Shakespeare does not walk the night. From hour to hour it rots and rots. He rests, disarmed of fatherhood, having devised that mystical estate upon his son. Boccaccio's Calandrino was the first and last man who felt himself with child. Fatherhood, in the sense of conscious begetting, is unknown to man. It is a mystical estate, an apostolic succession, from only begetter to only begotten. On that mystery and not on the madonna which the cunning Italian intellect flung to the mob of Europe the church is founded and founded irremovably because founded, like the world, macro- and microcosm, upon the void. Upon incertitude, upon unlikelihood. *Amor Matris*, subjective and objective genitive, may be the only true thing in life. Paternity may be a legal fiction. Who is the father of any son that any son should love him or he any son?

What the hell are you driving at?

I know. Shut up. Blast you! I have reasons.

Are you condemned to do this?

—They are sundered by a bodily shame so steadfast that the criminal annals of the world, stained with all other incests and bestialities, hardly record its breach. Sons with mothers, sires with daughters, lesbic sisters, loves that dare not speak their name, nephews with grandmothers, jailbirds with keyholes, queens with prize bulls. The sun unborn mars beauty: born, he brings pain, divides affection, increases care. He is a male: his growth is his father's decline, his youth his father's envy, his friend his father's enemy.

In rue Monsieur-le-Prince I thought it.

—What links them in nature? An instant of blind rut.

Am I father? If I were?

Shrunken uncertain hand.

—Sabellius, the African, subtlest heresiarch of all the beasts of the field, held that the Father was Himself His Own Son. The bulldog of Aquin, with whom no word shall be impossible, refutes him. Well: if the father who has not a son be not a father can the son who has not a father be a son? When Rutlandbaconsouthamptonshakespeare or another poet of the same name in the comedy of errors wrote *Hamlet* he was not the father of his own son merely but, being no more a son, he was and felt himself the father of all his race, the father of his own grandfather, the father of his unborn grandson who, by the same token, never was born for nature, as Mr Magee understands her, abhors perfection.

Eglintoneyes, quick with pleasure, looked up shybrightly. Gladly glancing, a merry puritan, through the twisted eglantine.

Flatter. Rarely. But Flatter.

—Himself his own father, Sonmulligan told himself. Wait. I am big with child. I have an unborn child in my brain. Pallas Athena! A play! The play's the thing! Let me parturiate!

He clasped his paunchbrow with both birthaiding hands.

—As for his family, Stephen said, his mother's name lives in the forest of Arden. Her death brought from him the scene with Volumnia in *Coriolanus*. His boyson's death is the deathscene of young Arthur in *King John*. Hamlet, the black prince, is Hamnet Shakespeare. Who the girls in *The Tempest*, in *Pericles*, in *Winter's Tale* are we know. Who Cleopatra, fleshpot of Egypt, and Cressid and Venus are we may guess. But there is another member of his family who is recorded.

—The plot thickens, John Eglinton said.

The quaker librarian, quaking, tiptoed in, quake, his mask, quake, with haste, quake, quack.

Door closed. Cell. Day.

They list. Three. They.

I you he they.

Come, mess.

He had three brothers, Gilbert, Edmund, Richard. Gilbert in his old age told some cavaliers he got a pass for nowt from Maister Gatherer one time mass he did and he seen his brud Maister Wull the playwriter up in Lunnon in a wrastling play wud a man on's back. The playhouse sausage filled Gilbert's soul. He is nowhere: but an Edmund and a Richard are recorded in the works of sweet William.

MAGEEGLINJOHN

Names! What's in a name?

BEST

That is my name, Richard, don't you know. I hope you are going to say a good word for Richard, don't you know, for my sake.

(*Laughter.*)

BUCK MULLIGAN

(*Piano, diminuendo.*)

> *Then outspoke medical Dick*
> *To his comrade medical Davy* . . .

STEPHEN

In his trinity of black Wills, the villain shakebags, Iago, Richard Crookback, Edmund in *King Lear*, two bear the wicked uncles' names. Nay, that last play was written or being written while his brother Edmund lay dying in Southwark.

BEST

I hope Edmund is going to catch it. I don't want Richard, my name . . .

(*Laughter.*)

QUAKERLYSTER

(*A tempo.*) But he that filches from me my good name . . .

STEPHEN

(*Stringendo.*) He has hidden his own name, a fair name, William, in the plays, a super here, a clown there, as a painter of old Italy set his face in a dark corner of his canvas.

He has revealed it in the sonnets where there is Will in overplus. Like John O'Gaunt his name is dear to him, as dear as the coat of arms he toadied for, on a bend sable a spear or steeled argent, honorificabilitudinitatibus, dearer than his glory of greatest shakescene in the country. What's in a name? That is what we ask ourselves in childhood when we write the name that we are told is ours. A star, a daystar, a firedrake rose at his birth. It shone by day in the heavens alone, brighter than Venus in the night, and by night it shone over delta in Cassiopeia, the recumbent constellation which is the signature of his initial among the stars. His eyes watched it, lowlying on the horizon, eastward of the bear, as he walked by the slumberous summer fields at midnight, returning from Shottery and from her arms.

Both satisfied. I too.

Don't tell them he was nine years old when it was quenched.

And from her arms.

Wait to be wooed and won. Ay, meacock. Who will woo you?

Read the skies. *Autontimerumenos. Bous Stephanoumenos.* Where's your configuration? Stephen, Stephen, cut the bread even. S. D.: *sua donna. Già: di lui. Gelindo risolve di non amar. S. D.*

—What is that, Mr. Dedalus? the quaker librarian asked. Was it a celestial phenomenon?

—A star by night, Stephen said, a pillar of the cloud by day.

What more's to speak?

Stephen looked on his hat, his stick, his boots.

Stephanos, my crown. My sword. His boots are spoiling the shape of my feet. Buy a pair. Holes in my socks. Handkerchief too.

—You make good use of the name, John Eglinton allowed. Your own name is strange enough. I suppose it explains your fantastical humour.

Me, Magee and Mulligan.

Fabulous artificer, the hawklike man. You flew. Whereto? Newhaven-Dieppe, steerage passenger. Paris and back. Lapwing. Icarus. *Pater, ait.* Seabedabbled, fallen, weltering. Lapwing you are. Lapwing he.

Mr Best's eagerquietly lifted his book to say:

—That's very interesting because that brother motive, don't you know, we find also in the old Irish myths. Just what you say. The three brothers Shakespeare. In Grimm too, don't you know, the fairytales. The third brother that marries the sleeping beauty and wins the best prize.

Best of Best brothers. Good, better, best.

The quaker librarian springhalted near.

—I should like to know, he said, which brother you . . . I understand you to suggest there was misconduct with one of the brothers . . . But perhaps I am anticipating?

He caught himself in the act: looked at all: refrained.

An attendant from the doorway called:

—Mr Lyster! Father Dineen wants . . .

—O! Father Dineen! Directly.

Swiftly rectly creaking rectly rectly he was rectly gone.

John Eglinton touched the foil.

—Come, he said. Let us hear what you have to say of Richard and Edmund. You kept them for the last, didn't you?

—In asking you to remember those two noble kinsmen nuncle Richie and nuncle Edmund, Stephen answered, I feel I am asking too much perhaps. A brother is as easily forgotten as an umbrella.

Lapwing.

Where is your brother? Apothecaries' hall. My
whetstone. Him, then Cranly, Mulligan: now these. Speech,
speech. But act. Act speech. They mock to try you. Act. Be
acted on.
Lapwing.
I am tired of my voice, the voice of Esau. My kingdom
for a drink.
Oh.
—You will say those names were already in the
chronicles from which he took the stuff of his plays. Why
did he take them rather than others? Richard, a whorseson
crookback, misbegotten, makes love to a widowed Ann
(what's in a name?), woos and wins her, a shoreson merry
widow. Richard the conqueror, third brother, came after
William the conquered. The other four acts of that play hang
limply from that first. Of all his kings Richard is the only
king unshielded by Shakespeare's reverence, the angel of the
world. Why is the underplot of *King Lear* in which Edmund
figures lifted out of Sidney's *Arcadia* and spatchcocked on to
a Celtic legend older than history?
—That was Will's way, John Eglinton defended. We
should not now combine a Norse saga with an excerpt from
a novel by George Meredith. *Que voulez-vous?* Moore
would say. He puts Bohemia on the seacoast and makes
Ulysses quote Aristotle.
—Why? Stephen answered himself. Because the theme
of the false or the usurping or the adulterous brother or all
three in one is to Shakespeare, what the poor is not, always
with him. The note of banishment, banishment from the
heart, banishment from home, sounds uninterruptedly from
The Two Gentlemen of Verona onward till Prospero breaks
his staff, buries it certain fathoms in the earth and drowns
his book. It doubles itself in the middle of his life, reflects
itself in another, repeats itself, protasis, epitasis, catastasis,

catastrophe. It repeats itself again when he is near the grave, when his married daughter Susan, chip of the old block, is accused of adultery. But it was the original sin that darkened his understanding, weakened his will and left in him a strong inclination to evil. The words are those of my lords bishops of Maynooth: an original sin and, like original sin, committed by another in whose sin he too has sinned. It is between the lines of his last written words, it is petrified on his tombstone under which her four bones are not to be laid. Age has not withered it. Beauty and peace have not done it away. It is in infinite variety everywhere in the world he has created, in *Much Ado about Nothing*, twice in *As You Like It*, in *The Tempest,* in *Hamlet*, in *Measure for Measure*, and in all the other plays which I have not read.

He laughed to free his mind from his mind's bondage.

Judge Eglinton summed up.

—The truth is midway, he affirmed. He is the ghost and the prince. He is all in all.

—He is, Stephen said. The boy of act one is the mature man of act five. All in all. In *Cymbeline*, in *Othello* he is bawd and cuckold. He acts and is acted on. Lover of an ideal or a perversion, like José he kills the real Carmen. His unremitting intellect is the hornmad Iago ceaselessly willing that the moor in him shall suffer.

—Cuckoo! Cuckoo! Cuck Mulligan clucked lewdly. O word of fear!

Dark dome received, reverbed.

—And what a character is Iago! undaunted John Eglinton exclaimed. When all is said Dumas fils (or is it Dumas père?) is right. After God Shakespeare has created most.

—Man delights him not nor woman neither, Stephen said. He returns after a life of absence to that spot of earth where he was born, where he has always been, man and boy, a silent witness and there, his journey of life ended, he plants his mulberrytree in the earth. Then dies. The motion is ended. Gravediggers bury Hamlet *père* and Hamlet *fils*. A king and a prince at last in death, with incidental music. And, what though murdered and betrayed, bewept by all frail tender hearts for, Dane or Dubliner, sorrow for the dead is the only husband from whom they refuse to be divorced. If you like the epilogue look long on it: prosperous Prospero, the good man rewarded, Lizzie, grandpa's lump of love, and nuncle Richie, the bad man taken off by poetic justice to the place where the bad niggers go. Strong curtain. He found in the world without as actual what was in his world within as possible. Maeterlinck says: *If Socrates leave his house today he will find the sage seated on his doorstep. If Judas go forth tonight it is to Judas his steps will tend.* Every life is many days, day after day. We walk through ourselves, meeting robbers, ghosts, giants, old men, young men, wives, widows, brothers-in-love. But always meeting ourselves. The playwright who wrote the folio of this world and wrote it badly (He gave us light first and the sun two days later), the lord of things as they are whom the most Roman of catholics call *dio boia*, hangman god, is doubtless all in all in all of us, ostler and butcher, and would be bawd and cuckold too but that in the economy of heaven, foretold by Hamlet, there are no more marriages, glorified man, an androgynous angel, being a wife unto himself.

—*Eureka!* Buck Mulligan cried. *Eureka!*

Suddenly happied he jumped up and reached in a stride John Eglinton's desk.

—May I? he said. The Lord has spoken to Malachi.

He began to scribble on a slip of paper.

Take some slips from the counter going out.

—Those who are married, Mr Best, douce herald, said, all save one, shall live. The rest shall keep as they are.

He laughed, unmarried, at Eglinton Johannes, of arts a bachelor.

Unwed, unfancied, ware of wiles, they fingerponder nightly each his variorum edition of *The Taming of the Shrew*.

—You are a delusion, said roundly John Eglinton to Stephen. You have brought us all this way to show us a French triangle. Do you believe your own theory?

—No, Stephen said promptly.

—Are you going to write it? Mr Best asked. You ought to make it a dialogue, don't you know, like the Platonic dialogues Wilde wrote.

John Eclecticon doubly smiled.

—Well, in that case, he said, I don't see why you should expect payment for it since you don't believe it yourself. Dowden believes there is some mystery in *Hamlet* but will say no more. Herr Bleibtreu, the man Piper met in Berlin, who is working up that Rutland theory, believes that the secret is hidden in the Stratford monument. He is going to visit the present duke, Piper says, and prove to him that his ancestor wrote the plays. It will come as a surprise to his grace. But he believes his theory.

I believe, O Lord, help my unbelief. That is, help me to believe or help me to unbelieve? Who helps to believe? *Egomen*. Who to unbelieve? Other chap.

—You are the only contributor to *Dana* who asks for pieces of silver. Then I don't know about the next number. Fred Ryan wants space for an article on economics.

Fraidrine. Two pieces of silver he lent me. Tide you over. Economics.

—For a guinea, Stephen said, you can publish this interview.

Buck Mulligan stood up from his laughing scribbling, laughing: and then gravely said, honeying malice:

—I called upon the bard Kinch at his summer residence in upper Mecklenburgh street and found him deep in the study of the *Summa contra Gentiles* in the company of two gonorrheal ladies, Fresh Nelly and Rosalie, the coalquay whore.

He broke away.

—Come, Kinch. Come, wander Ængus of the birds.

Come, Kinch, you have eaten all we left. Ay, I will serve you your orts and offals.

Stephen rose.

Life is many days. This will end.

—We shall see you tonight, John Eglinton said. *Notre ami* Moore says Malachi Mulligan must be there.

Buck Mulligan flaunted his slip and panama.

—Monsieur Moore, he said, lecturer on French letters to the youth of Ireland. I'll be there. Come, Kinch, the bards must drink. Can you walk straight?

Laughing he . . .

Swill till eleven. Irish nights' entertainment.

Lubber . . .

Stephen followed a lubber . . .

One day in the national library we had a discussion. Shakes. After his lub back I followed. I gall his kibe.

Stephen, greeting, then all amort, followed a lubber jester, a wellkempt head, newbarbered, out of the vaulted cell into a shattering daylight of no thoughts.

What have I learned? Of them? Of me?

Walk like Haines now.

The constant readers' room. In the readers' book Cashel Boyle O'Connor Fitzmaurice Tisdall Farrell parades his polysyllables. Item: was Hamlet mad? The quaker's pate godlily with a priesteen in booktalk.

—O please do, sir . . . I shall be most pleased . . .

Amused Buck Mulligan mused in pleasant murmur with himself, selfnodding:

—A pleased bottom.

The turnstile.

Is that? . . . Blueribboned hat . . . Idly writing . . . What? Looked? . . .

The curving balustrade; smoothsliding Mincius.

Puck Mulligan, panamahelmeted, went step by step, iambing, trolling:

> *John Eglinton, my jo, John.*
> *Why won't you wed a wife?*

He sputtered to the air:

—O, the chinless Chinaman! Chin Chon Eg Lin Ton. We went over to their playbox, Haines and I, the plumbers' hall. Our players are creating a new art for Europe like the Greeks or M. Maeterlinck. Abbey theatre! I smell the public sweat of monks.

He spat blank.

Forgot: any more than he forgot the whipping lousy Lucy gave him. And left the *femme de trente ans.* And why no other children born? And his first child a girl?

Afterwit. Go back.

ROSENCRANTZ AND GUILDENSTERN ARE DEAD

Tom Stoppard

ROS *goes upstage: Ideally a sort of upper deck joined to the downstage lower deck by short steps. The umbrella being on the upper deck.* ROS *pauses by the umbrella and looks behind it.* GUIL *meanwhile has been resuming his own theme—looking out over the audience——*

Free to move, speak, extemporise, and yet. We have not been cut loose. Our truancy is defined by one fixed star, and our drift represents merely a slight change of angle to it: we may seize the moment, toss it around while the moments pass, a short dash here, an exploration there, but we are brought round full circle to face again the single immutable fact—that we, Rosencrantz and Guildenstern, bearing a letter from one king to another, are taking Hamlet to England.

By which time, ROS *has returned, tiptoeing with great import, teeth clenched for secrecy, gets to* GUIL, *points surreptitiously behind him—and a tight whisper:*

ROS: I say—*he's there!*

GUIL (*unsurprised*): What's he doing?

ROS: Sleeping.

GUIL: It's all right for him.

ROS: What is?

GUIL: He can sleep.

ROS: It's all right for him .

GUIL: He's got us now.

ROS: He can sleep.

GUIL: It's all done for him.

ROS: He's got us.

GUIL: And we've got nothing. (*A cry.*) All I ask is our common due!

ROS: For those in peril on the sea. . . .

GUIL: Give us this day our daily cue.

Beat, pause. Sit. Long pause.

ROS (*after shifting, looking around*): What now?

GUIL: What do you mean?

ROS: Well, nothing is happening.

GUIL: We're on a boat.

ROS: I'm aware of that.

GUIL (*angrily*): Then what do you expect? (*Unhappily.*) We act on scraps of information . . . sifting half-remembered directions that we can hardly separate from instinct.

ROS *puts a hand into his purse, then both hands behind his back, then holds his fists out.*

GUIL *taps one fist.*

ROS *opens it to show a coin.*

He gives it to GUIL.

He puts his hand back into his purse. Then both hands behind his back, then holds his fists out.

GUIL *taps one.*

ROS *opens it to show a coin. He gives it to* GUIL.

Repeat.

Repeat.

GUIL *getting tense. Desperate to lose.*

Repeat.

GUIL *taps a hand, changes his mind, taps the other, and* ROS *inadvertently reveals that he has a coin in both fists.*

GUIL: You had money in both hands.

ROS (*embarrassed*): Yes.

GUIL: Every time?

ROS: Yes.

GUIL: What's the point of that?

ROS (*pathetic*): I wanted to make you happy.

Beat.

GUIL: How much did he give you?

ROS: Who?

GUIL: The King. He gave us some money.

ROS: How much did he give you?

GUIL: I asked you first.

ROS: I got the same as you.

GUIL: He wouldn't discriminate between us.

ROS: How much did you get?

GUIL: The same.

ROS: How do you know?

GUIL: You just told me—how do *you* know?

ROS: He wouldn't discriminate between us.

GUIL: Even if he could.

ROS: Which he never could.

GUIL: He couldn't even be sure of mixing us up.

ROS: Without mixing us up.

GUIL (*turning on him furiously*): Why don't you say something original! No wonder the whole thing is so stagnant! You don't take me up on anything—you just repeat it in a different order.

ROS: I can't think of anything original. I'm only good in support.

GUIL: I'm sick of making the running.

ROS (*humbly*): It must be your dominant personality. (*Almost in tears.*) Oh, what's going to become of us!

And GUIL *comforts him, all harshness gone.*

GUIL: Don't cry . . . it's all right . . . there . . . there, I'll see we're all right.

ROS: But we've got nothing to go on, we're out on our own.

GUIL: We're on our way to England—we're taking Hamlet there.

ROS: What for?

GUIL: What for? Where have you been?

ROS: When? (*Pause.*) We won't know what to do when we get there.

GUIL: We take him to the King.

ROS: Will *he* be there?

GUIL: No—the king of England.

ROS: He's expecting us?

GUIL: No.

ROS: He won't know what we're playing at. What are we going to *say*?

GUIL: We've got a letter. You remember the letter.

ROS: Do I?

GUIL: Everything is explained in the letter. We count on that.

ROS: Is that it, then?

GUIL: What?

ROS: We take Hamlet to the English king, we hand over the letter—what then?

GUIL: There may be something in the letter to keep us going a bit.

ROS: And if not?

GUIL: Then that's it—we're finished.

ROS: At a loose end?

GUIL: Yes.

Pause.

ROS: Are there likely to be loose ends? (*Pause.*) Who is the English king?

GUIL: That depends on when we get there.

ROS: What do you think it says?

GUIL: Oh . . . greetings. Expressions of loyalty. Asking of favours, calling in of debts. Obscure promises balanced by vague threats. . . . Diplomacy. Regards to the family.

ROS: And about Hamlet?

GUIL: Oh yes.

ROS: And us—the full background?

GUIL: I should say so.

Pause.

ROS: So we've got a letter which explains everything.

GUIL: You've got it.

ROS *takes that literally. He starts to pat his pockets, etc.*

What's the matter?

ROS: The letter.

GUIL: Have you got it?

ROS (*rising fear*): Have I? (*Searches frantically.*) Where would I have put it?

GUIL: You can't have lost it.

ROS: I must have!

GUIL: That's odd—I thought he gave it to me.

ROS *looks at him hopefully.*

ROS: Perhaps he did.

GUIL: But you seemed so sure it was *you* who hadn't got it.

ROS (*high*): It *was* me who hadn't got it!

GUIL: But if he gave it to me there's no reason why you should have had it in the first place, in which case I don't see what all the fuss is about you *not* having it.

ROS (*pause*): I admit it's confusing.

GUIL: This is all getting rather undisciplined. . . . The boat, the night, the sense of isolation and uncertainty . . . all these induce a loosening of the concentration. We must not lose control. Tighten up. Now. Either you have lost the letter or you didn't have it to lose in the first place, in which case the King never gave it to you, in which case he gave it to me, in which case I would have put it into my inside top pocket, in which case (*calmly producing the letter*) . . . it will be . . . here. (*They smile at each other.*) We mustn't drop off like that again.

Pause. ROS *takes the letter gently from him.*

ROS: Now that we have found it, why were we looking for it?

GUIL (*thinks*): We thought it was lost.

ROS: Something else?

GUIL: No.

Deflation.

ROS: Now we've lost the tension.

GUIL: What tension?

ROS: What was the last thing I said before we wandered off?

GUIL: When was that?

ROS (*helplessly*): I can't remember.

GUIL (*leaping up*): What a shambles! We're just not getting anywhere.

ROS (*mournfully*): Not even England. I don't believe in it anyway.

GUIL: What?

ROS: England.

GUIL: Just a conspiracy of cartographers, you mean?

ROS: I mean I don't believe it! (*Calmer.*) I have no image. I try to picture us arriving, a little harbour perhaps . . . roads . . . inhabitants to point the way . . . horses on the road . . . riding for a day or a fortnight and then a palace and the English king. . . . That would be the logical kind of thing. . . . But my mind remains a blank. No. We're slipping off the map.

GUIL: Yes . . . yes. . . . (*Rallying.*) But you don't believe anything till it happens. And it *has* all happened. Hasn't it?

ROS: We drift down time, clutching at straws. But what good's a brick to a drowning man?

GUIL: Don't give up, we can't be long now.

ROS: We might as well be dead. Do you think death could possibly be a boat?

GUIL: No, no, no . . . Death is . . . not. Death isn't. You take my meaning. Death is the ultimate negative. Not-being. You can't not-be on a boat.

ROS: I've frequently not been on boats.

GUIL: No, no, no—what you've been is not on boats.

ROS: I wish I was dead. (*Considers the drop.*) I could jump over the side. That would put a spoke in their wheel.

GUIL: Unless they're counting on it.

ROS: I shall remain on board. That'll put a spoke in their wheel. (*The futility of it, fury.*) All right! We don't question, we don't doubt. We perform. But a line must be drawn somewhere, and I would like to put it on record that I have no confidence in England. Thank you. (*Thinks about this.*) And even if it's true, it'll just be another shambles.

GUIL: I don't see why.

ROS (*furious*): He won't know what we're talking about.— What are we going to *say*?

GUIL: We say—Your majesty, we have arrived!

ROS: (*kingly*): And who are you?

GUIL: We are Rosencrantz and Guildenstern.

ROS (*barks*): Never heard of you!

GUIL: Well, we're nobody special——

ROS (*regal and nasty*): What's your game?

GUIL: We've got our instructions——

ROS: First I've heard of it——

GUIL (*angry*): Let me finish—— (*Humble.*) We've come from Denmark.

ROS: What do you want?

GUIL: Nothing—we're delivering Hamlet——

ROS: Who's he?

GUIL (*irritated*): You've heard of *him*——

ROS: Oh, I've heard of him all right and I want nothing to do with it.

GUIL: But——

ROS: You march in here without so much as a by-your-leave and expect me to take in every lunatic you try to pass off with a lot of unsubstantiated——

GUIL: We've got a letter——

ROS *snatches it and tears it open.*

ROS (*efficiently*): I see . . . I see . . . well, this seems to support your story such as it is—it is an exact command from the king of Denmark, for several different reasons, importing Denmark's health and England's too, that on the reading of this letter, without delay, I should have Hamlet's head cut off——!

GUIL *snatches the letter.* ROS, *double-taking, snatches it back.* GUIL *snatches it half back. They read it together, and separate.*

Pause.

They are well downstage looking front.

ROS: The sun's going down. It will be dark soon.

GUIL: Do you think so?

ROS: I was just making conversation. (*Pause.*) We're his *friends.*

GUIL: How do you know?

ROS: From our young days brought up with him.

GUIL: You've only got their word for it.

ROS: But that's what we depend on.

GUIL: Well, yes, and then again no. (*Airily.*) Let us keep things in proportion. Assume, if you like, that they're going to kill him. Well, he is a man, he is mortal, death comes to us all, etcetera, and consquently he would have died anyway, sooner or later. Or to look at it from the social point of view—he's just one man among many, the loss would be well within reason and convenience. And then again, what is so terrible about death? As Socrates so philosophically put it, since we don't know what death is, it is illogical to fear it. It might be . . . very nice. Certainly it is a release from the burden of life, and, for the godly, a haven and a reward. Or to look at it another way—we are little men, we don't know the ins and outs of the matter, there are wheels within wheels, etcetera—it would be presumptuous of us to interfere with the designs of fate or even of kings. All in all, I think we'd be well advised to leave well alone. Tie up the letter—there—neatly—like that.—They won't notice the broken seal, assuming you were in character.

ROS: But what's the point?

GUIL: Don't apply logic.

ROS: He's done nothing to us.

GUIL: Or justice.

ROS: It's awful.

GUIL: But it could have been worse. I was beginning to think it was. (*And his relief comes out in a laugh.*)

Behind them HAMLET *appears from behind the umbrella. The light has been going. Slightly.* HAMLET *is going to the lantern.*

ROS: The position as I see it, then. We, Rosencrantz and Guildenstern, from our young days brought up with him, awakened by a man standing on his saddle, are summoned, and arrive, and are instructed to glean what afflicts him and draw him on to pleasures, such as a play, which unfortunately, as it turns out, is abandoned in some confusion owing to certain nuances outside our appreciation—which, among other causes, results in, among other effects, a high, not to say, homicidal, excitement in Hamlet, whom we, in consequence, are escorting, for his own good, to England. Good. We're on top of it now.

HAMLET *blows out the lantern. The stage goes pitch black. The black resolves itself to moonlight, by which* HAMLET *approaches the sleeping* ROS *and* GUIL. *He extracts the letter and takes it behind his umbrella; the light of his lantern shines through the fabric,* HAMLET *emerges again with a letter, and replaces it, and retires, blowing out his lantern.*

Morning comes.

ROS *watches it coming—from the auditorium. Behind him is a gay sight. Beneath the re-tilted umbrella, reclining in a deck-chair, wrapped in a rug, reading a book, possibly smoking, sits* HAMLET.

ROS *watches the morning come, and brighten to high noon.*

ROS: I'm assuming nothing. (*He stands up.* GUIL *wakes.*) The position as I see it, then. That's west unless we're off course, in which case it's night; the King gave me the same as you, the King gave you the same as me; the King never gave me the letter, the King gave you the letter, we don't know what's in the letter; we take Hamlet to the English king, it depending on when we get there who he is, and we hand over the letter, which may or may not have something

in it to keep us going, and if not, we are finished and at a
loose end, if they have loose ends. We could have done
worse. I don't think we missed any chances. . . . Not that
we're getting much help. (*He sits down again. They lie
down—prone.*) If we stopped breathing we'd vanish.

*The muffled sound of a recorder. They sit up with
disproportionate interest.*

GUIL: Here we go.

ROS: Yes, but what?

They listen to the music.

GUIL (*excitedly*): Out of the void, finally, a sound; while on
a boat (admittedly) outside the action (admittedly) the perfect
and absolute silence of the wet lazy slap of water against
water and the rolling creak of timber—breaks; giving rise at
once to the speculation or the assumption or the hope that
something is about to happen; a pipe is heard. One of the
sailors has pursed his lips against a woodwind, his fingers
and thumb governing, shall we say, the ventages,
whereupon, giving it breath, let us say, with his mouth, it,
the pipe, discourses, as the saying goes, most eloquent
music. A thing like that, it could change the course of
events. (*Pause.*) Go and see what it is.

ROS: It's someone playing on a pipe.

GUIL: Go and find him.

ROS: And then what?

GUIL: I don't know—request a tune.

ROS: What for?

GUIL: Quick—before we lose our momentum.

ROS: Why!—something is happening. It had quite escaped my attention!

He listens: Makes a stab at an exit. Listens more carefully: Changes direction.

GUIL *takes no notice.*

ROS *wanders about trying to decide where the music comes from. Finally he tracks it down—unwillingly—to the middle barrel. There is no getting away from it. He turns to* GUIL *who takes no notice.* ROS, *during this whole business, never quite breaks into articulate speech. His face and his hands indicate his incredulity. He stands gazing at the middle barrel. The pipe plays on within. He kicks the barrel. The pipe stops. He leaps back towards* GUIL. *The pipe starts up again. He approaches the barrel cautiously. He lifts the lid. The music is louder. He slams down the lid. The music is softer. He goes back towards* GUIL. *But a drum starts, muffled. He freezes. He turns. Considers the left-hand barrel. The drumming goes on within, in time to the flute. He walks back to* GUIL. *He opens his mouth to speak. Doesn't make it. A lute is heard. He spins round at the third barrel. More instruments join in. Until it is quite inescapable that inside the three barrels, distributed, playing together a familiar tune which has been heard three times before, are the* TRAGEDIANS.

They play on.

ROS *sits beside* GUIL. *They stare ahead.*

The tune comes to an end.

Pause.

ROS: I thought I heard a band. (*In anguish.*) Plausibility is all I presume!

GUIL (*coda*): Call us this day our daily tune. . . .

The lid of the middle barrel flies open and the PLAYER'*s head pops out.*

PLAYER: Aha! All in the same boat, then! (*He climbs out. He goes round banging on the barrels.*)

Everybody out!

Impossibly, the TRAGEDIANS *climb out of the barrels. With their instruments, but not their cart. A few bundles. Except* ALFRED. *The* PLAYER *is cheerful.*

(*To* ROS:) Where are we?

ROS: Travelling.

PLAYER: Of course, we haven't got there yet.

ROS: Are we all right for England?

PLAYER: You look all right to me. I don't think they're very particular in England. Al-l-fred!

ALFRED *emerges from the* PLAYER's *barrel.*

GUIL: What are you doing here?

PLAYER: Travelling. (*To* TRAGEDIANS:) Right—blend into the background!

The TRAGEDIANS *are in costume (from the mime): A King with crown,* ALFRED *as Queen, Poisoner and the two cloaked figures.*

They blend.

(*To* GUIL:) Pleased to see us? (*Pause.*) You've come out of it very well, so far.

GUIL: And you?

PLAYER: In disfavour. Our play offended the King.

GUIL: Yes.

PLAYER: Well, he's a second husband himself. Tactless, really.

ROS: It was quite a good play nevertheless.

PLAYER: We never really got going—it was getting quite interesting when they stopped it.

Looks up at HAMLET.

That's the way to travel. . . .

GUIL: What were you doing in there?

PLAYER: Hiding. (*Indicating costumes.*) We had to run for it just as we were.

ROS: Stowaways.

PLAYER: Naturally—we didn't get paid, owing to circumstances ever so slightly beyond our control, and all the money we had we lost betting on certainties. Life is a gamble, at terrible odds—if it was a bet you wouldn't take it. Did you know that any number doubled is even?

ROS: Is it?

PLAYER: We learn something every day, to our cost. But we troupers just go on and on. Do you know what happens to old actors?

ROS: What?

PLAYER: Nothing. They're still acting. Surprised, then?

GUIL: What?

PLAYER: Surprised to see us?

GUIL: I knew it wasn't the end.

PLAYER: With practically everyone on his feet. What do you make of it, so far?

GUIL: We haven't got much to go on.

PLAYER: You speak to him?

ROS: It's possible.

GUIL: But it wouldn't make any difference.

ROS: But it's possible.

GUIL: Pointless.

ROS: It's allowed.

GUIL: Allowed, yes. We are not restricted. No boundaries have been defined, no inhibitions imposed. We have, for the while, secured, or blundered into, our release, for the while. Spontaneity and whim are the order of the day. Other wheels are turning but they are not our concern. We can breathe. We can relax. We can do what we like and say what we like to whomever we like, without restriction.

ROS: Within limits, of course.

GUIL: Certainly within limits.

HAMLET *comes down to footlights and regards the audience. The others watch but don't speak.* HAMLET clears his throat noisily and spits into the audience. A split second later he claps his hand to his eye and wipes himself. He goes back upstage.

ROS: A compulsion towards philosophical introspection is his chief characteristic, if I may put it like that. It does not mean he is mad. It does not mean he isn't. Very often, it does not mean anything at all. Which may or may not be a kind of madness.

GUIL: It really boils down to symptoms. Pregnant replies, mystic allusions, mistaken identities, arguing his father is his mother, that sort of thing; intimations of suicide, forgoing of exercise, loss of mirth, hints of claustrophobia not to say delusions of imprisonment; invocations of camels, chameleons, capons, whales, weasels, hawks, handsaws—riddles, quibbles and evasions; amnesia, paranoia, myopia; day-dreaming, hallucinations; stabbing his elders, abusing his parents, insulting his lover, and appearing hatless in public—knock-kneed, droop-stockinged and sighing like a love-sick schoolboy, which at his age is coming on a bit strong.

ROS: And talking to himself.

GUIL: And talking to himself.

ROS *and* GUIL *move apart together.*

Well, where has that got us?

ROS: He's the Player.

GUIL: His play offended the King——

ROS: —offended the King——

GUIL: —who orders his arrest——

ROS: —orders his arrest——

GUIL: —so he escapes to England——

ROS: On the boat to which he meets——

GUIL: Guildenstern and Rosencratz taking Hamlet——

ROS: —who also offended the King——

GUIL: —and killed Polonius——

ROS: —offended the King in a variety of ways——

GUIL: —to England. (*Pause.*) That seems to be it.

ROS *jumps up.*

ROS: Incidents! All we get is incidents! Dear God, is it too much to expect a little sustained action?!

And on the word, the PIRATES *attack. That is to say: Noise and shouts and rushing about. "Pirates."*

Everyone visible goes frantic. HAMLET *draws his sword and rushes downstage.* GUIL, ROS *and* PLAYER *draw swords and rush upstage. Collision.* HAMLET *turns back up. They turn back down. Collision. By which time there is general panic right upstage. All four charge upstage with* ROS, GUIL *and* PLAYER *shouting:*

> At last!
> To arms!
> Pirates!
> Up there!

> Down there!
> To my sword's length!
> Action!

All four reach the top, see something they don't like, waver, run for their lives downstage:

HAMLET, *in the lead, leaps into the left barrel.* PLAYER *leaps into the right barrel.* ROS *and* GUIL *leap into the middle barrel. All closing the lids after them.*

*The lights dim to nothing while the sound of fighting continues. The sound fades to nothing. The lights come up. The middle barrel (*ROS's *and* GUIL's*) is missing.*

The lid of the right-hand barrel is raised cautiously, the heads of ROS *and* GUIL *appear.*

*The lid of the other barrel (*HAMLET's *is raised. The head of the* PLAYER *appears.*

All catch sight of each other and slam down lids.

Pause.

Lids raised cautiously.

ROS (*relief*): They've gone. (*He starts to climb out.*) That was close. I've never thought quicker.

They are all three out of barrels. GUIL *is wary and nervous.* ROS *is light-headed. The* PLAYER *is phlegmatic. They note the missing barrel.*

ROS *looks round.*

ROS: Where's———?

The PLAYER *takes off his hat in mourning.*

PLAYER: Once more, alone—on our own resources.

GUIL (*worried*): What do you mean? Where is he?

PLAYER: Gone.

GUIL: Gone where?

PLAYER: Yes, we were dead lucky there. If that's the word I'm after.

ROS (*not a pick up*): Dead?

PLAYER: Lucky.

ROS (*he means*): Is he dead?

PLAYER: Who knows?

GUIL (*rattled*): He's not coming back?

PLAYER: Hardly.

ROS: He's dead then. He's dead as far as we're concerned.

PLAYER: Or we are as far as he is. (*He goes and sits on the floor to one side.*) Not too bad, is it?

GUIL (*rattled*): But he can't—we're supposed to be—we've got a *letter*—we're going to England with a letter for the King——

PLAYER: Yes, that much seems certain. I congratulate you on the unambiguity of your situation.

GUIL: But you don't understand—it contains—we've had our instructions—the whole thing's pointless without him.

PLAYER: Pirates could happen to anyone. Just deliver the letter. They'll send ambassadors from England to explain. . . .

GUIL (*worked up*): Can't you see—the pirates left us home and high—dry and home—drome——(*Furiously.*) The pirates left us high and dry!

PLAYER (*comforting*): There . . .

GUIL (*near tears*): Nothing will be resolved without him. . . .

PLAYER: There . . . !

GUIL: We need Hamlet for our release!

PLAYER: There!

GUIL: What are we supposed to do?

PLAYER: This.

He turns away, lies down if he likes. ROS *and* GUIL *apart.*
ROS: Saved again.

GUIL: Saved for what?

ROS *sighs.*

ROS: The sun's going down. (*Pause.*) It'll be night soon. (*Pause.*) If that's west. (*Pause.*) Unless we've——

GUIL (*shouts*): Shut up! I'm sick of it! Do you think conversation is going to help us now?

ROS (*hurt, desperately ingratiating*): I—I bet you all the money I've got the year of my birth doubled is an odd number.

GUIL (*moan*): No-o.

ROS: *Your* birth!

GUIL *smashes him down.*

GUIL (*broken*): We've travelled too far, and our momentum has taken over; we move idly towards eternity, without possibility of reprieve or hope of explanation.

ROS: Be happy—if you're not even *happy* what's so good about surviving? (*He picks himself up.*) We'll be all right. I suppose we just go on.

GUIL: Go where?

ROS: To England.

GUIL: England! *That's* a dead end. I never believed in it anyway.

ROS: All we've got to do is make our report and that'll be that. Surely.

GUIL: I don't *believe* it—a shore, a harbour, say—and we get off and we stop someone and say—Where's the King?— And he says, Oh, you follow that road there and take the first left and——(*Furiously.*) I don't believe any of it!

ROS: It doesn't sound very plausible.

GUIL: And even if we came face to face, what do we say?

ROS: We say—We've arrived!

GUIL (*kingly*): And who are you?

ROS: We are Guildenstern and Rosencrantz.

GUIL: Which is which?

ROS: Well, I'm—You're——

GUIL: What's it all about?——

ROS: Well, we were bringing Hamlet—but then some pirates——

GUIL: I don't begin to understand. Who are all these people, what's it got to do with me? You turn up out of the blue with some cock and bull story——

ROS (*with letter*): We have a letter——

GUIL (*snatches it, opens it*): A letter—yes—that's true. That's something . . . a letter . . . (*Reads.*) "As England is Denmark's faithful tributary . . . as love between them like the palm might flourish, etcetera . . . that on the knowing of this contents, without delay of any kind, should those bearers, Rosencrantz and Guildenstern, put to sudden death——"

He double-takes. ROS *snatches the letter.* GUIL *snatches it back.* ROS *snatches it half back. They read it again and look up.*

The PLAYER *gets to his feet and walks over to his barrel and kicks it and shouts into it.*

PLAYER: They've gone! It's all over!

One by one the PLAYERS *emerge, impossibly, from the barrel, and form a casually menacing circle round* ROS *and* GUIL, *who are still appalled and mesmerised.*

GUIL (*quietly*): Where we went wrong was getting on a boat. We can move, of course, change direction, rattle about, but our movement is contained within a larger one that carries us along as inexorably as the wind and current. . . .

ROS: They had it in for us, didn't they? Right from the beginning. Who'd have thought that we were so important?

GUIL: But why? Was it all for this? Who are we that so much should converge on our little deaths? (*In anguish to the* PLAYER:) Who are *we*?

PLAYER: You are Rosencrantz and Guildenstern. That's enough.

GUIL: No—it is not enough. To be told so little—to such an end—and still, finally, to be denied an explanation——

PLAYER: In our experience, most things end in death.

GUIL (*fear, vengeance, scorn*): Your experience!—*Actors!*

He snatches a dagger from the PLAYER's *belt and holds the point at the* PLAYER's *throat: the* PLAYER *backs and* GUIL *advances, speaking more quietly.*

I'm talking about death—and you've never experienced *that.* And you cannot *act* it. You die a thousand casual deaths— with none of that intensity which squeezes out life . . . and no blood runs cold anywhere. Because even as you die you know that you will come back in a different hat. But no one gets up after *death*—there is no applause—there is only silence and some second-hand clothes, and that's—*death*——

And he pushes the blade in up to the hilt. The PLAYER *stands with huge, terrible eyes, clutches at the wound as the blade withdraws: he makes small weeping sounds and falls to his knees, and then right down.*

While he is dying, GUIL, *nervous, high, almost hysterical, wheels on the* TRAGEDIANS—

If we have a destiny, then so had he—and if this is ours, then that was his—and if there are no explanations for us, then let there be none for him——

The TRAGEDIANS *watch the* PLAYER *die: they watch with some interest. The* PLAYER *finally lies still. A short moment of silence. Then the* TRAGEDIANS *start to applaud with genuine admiration. The* PLAYER *stands up, brushing himself down.*

PLAYER (*modestly*): Oh, come, come, gentlemen—no flattery—it was merely competent——

The TRAGEDIANS *are still congratulating him. The* PLAYER *approaches* GUIL, *who stand rooted, holding the dagger.*

PLAYER: What did you think? (*Pause.*) You see, it *is* the kind they do believe in—it's what is expected.

He holds his hand out for the dagger. GUIL *slowly puts the point of the dagger on to the* PLAYER's *hand, and pushes . . . the blade slides back into the handle. The* PLAYER *smiles, reclaims the dagger.*

For a moment you thought I'd—cheated.

ROS *relieves his own tension with loud nervy laughter.*

ROS: Oh, very good! *Very* good! Took me in completely— didn't he take you in completely—(*claps his hands*). Encore! Encore!

PLAYER (*activated, arms spread, the professional*): Deaths for all ages and occasions! Deaths by suspension, convulsion, consumption, incision, execution, asphyxiation and malnutrition—! Climactic carnage, by poison and by steel—! Double deaths by duel—! Show!—

ALFRED, *still in his Queen's costume, dies by poison: the*
PLAYER, *with rapier, kills the* "KING" *and duels with a
fourth* TRAGEDIAN, *inflicting and receiving a wound. The
two remaining* TRAGEDIANS, *the two* "SPIES" *dressed in the
same coats as* ROS *and* GUIL, *are stabbed, as before. And
the light is fading over the deaths which take place right
upstage.*

(*Dying amid the dying—tragically; romantically.*) So there's
an end to that—it's commonplace: light goes with life, and in
the winter of your years the dark comes early. . . .

GUIL (*tired, drained, but still an edge of impatience; over the
mime*): No . . . no . . . not for *us*, not like that. Dying is not
romantic, and death is not a game which will soon be
over . . . Death is not anything . . . death is not . . . It's the
absence of presence, nothing more . . . the endless time of
never coming back . . . a gap you can't see, and when the
wind blows through it, it makes no sound. . . .

The light has gone upstage. Only GUIL *and* ROS *are visible
as* ROS's *clapping falters to silence.*

Small pause.

ROS: That's it, then, is it?

No answer. He looks out front.

The sun's going down. Or the earth's coming up, as the
fashionable theory has it.

Small pause.

Not that it makes any difference.

Pause.

What was it all about? When did it begin?

Pause. No answer.

Couldn't we just stay put? I mean no one is going to come on and drag us off. . . . They'll just have to wait. We're still young . . . fit . . . we've got years. . . .

Pause. No answer.

(*A cry.*) We've done nothing wrong! We didn't harm anyone. Did we?

GUIL: I can't remember.

ROS *pulls himself together.*

ROS: All right, then. I don't care. I've had enough. To tell you the truth, I'm relieved.

And he disappears from view. GUIL *does not notice.*

GUIL: Our names shouted in a certain dawn . . . a message. . . a summons . . . There must have been a moment, at the beginning, where we could have said—no. But somehow we missed it. (*He looks round and sees he is alone.*)

Rosen—?
Guil—?

He gathers himself.

Well, we'll know better next time. Now you see me, now
you—(*and disappears*).

*Immediately the whole stage is lit up, revealing, upstage,
arranged in the approximate positions last held by the dead*
TRAGEDIANS, *the tableau of court and corpses which is the
last scene of* Hamlet.

That is: The KING, QUEEN, LAERTES *and* HAMLET *all dead.*
HORATIO *holds* HAMLET. FORTINBRAS *is there.*

So are two AMBASSADORS *from England.*

AMBASSADOR: The sight is dismal;
and our affairs from England come too late.
The ears are senseless that should give us hearing
to tell him his commandment is fulfilled,
that Rosencrantz and Guildenstern are dead.
Where should we have our thanks?

HORATIO: Not from his mouth,
had it the ability of life to thank you;
      He never gave commandment for their death.
But since, so jump upon this bloody question,
you from the Polack wars, and you from England,
are here arrived, give order that these bodies
high on a stage be placed to the view;
and let me speak to the yet unknowing world
      how these things came about: so shall you hear
of carnal, bloody and unnatural acts,
of accidental judgments, casual slighters,
of deaths put on by cunning and forced cause,

and, in this upshot, purposes mistook
fallen on the inventors' heads: all this can I
truly deliver.

*But during the above speech, the play fades out, overtaken
by dark and music.*

BUT SOFT . . . REAL SOFT

Woody Allen

Ask the average man who wrote the plays entitled *Hamlet*, *Romeo and Juliet, King Lear*, and *Othello*, and in most cases he'll snap confidently back with, "The Immortal Bard of Stratford on Avon." Ask him about the authorship of the Shakespearean sonnets and see if you don't get the same illogical reply. Now put these questions to certain literary detectives who seem to crop up every now and again over the years, and don't be surprised if you get answers like Sir Francis Bacon, Ben Jonson, Queen Elizabeth and possibly even the Homestead Act.

The most recent of these theories is to be found in a book I have just read that attempts to prove conclusively that the real author of Shakespeare's works was Christopher Marlowe. The book makes a very convincing case, and when I got through reading it I was not sure if Shakespeare was Marlowe or Marlowe was Shakespeare or what. I know this, I would not have cashed checks for either one of them—and I like their work.

Now, in trying to keep the above mentioned theory in perspective, my first question is: if Marlowe wrote Shakespeare's works, who wrote Marlowe's? The answer to this lies in the fact that Shakespeare was married to a woman named Anne Hathaway. This we know to be factual. However, under the new theory, it is actually Marlowe who was married to Anne Hathaway, a match which caused Shakespeare no end of grief, as they would not let him in the house.

One fateful day, in a jealous rage over who held the lower number in a bakery, Marlowe was slain—slain or whisked away in disguise to avoid charges of heresy, a most serious crime punishable by slaying or whisking away or both.

It was at this point that Marlowe's young wife took up the pen and continued to write the plays and sonnets we all know and avoid today. But allow me to clarify.

We all realize Shakespeare (Marlowe) borrowed his plots from the ancients (moderns); however, when the time came to return the plots to the ancients he had used them up and was forced to flee the country under the assumed name of William Bard (hence the term "immortal bard") in an effort to avoid debtor's prison (hence the term "debtor's prison"). Here Sir Francis Bacon enters into the picture. Bacon was an innovator of the times who was working on advanced concepts of refrigeration. Legend has it he died attempting to refrigerate a chicken. Apparently the chicken pushed first. In an effort to conceal Marlowe from Shakespeare, should they prove to be the same person, Bacon had adopted the fictitious name Alexander Pope, who in reality was Pope Alexander, head of the Roman Catholic Church and currently in exile owing to the invasion of Italy by the Bards, last of the nomadic hordes (the Bards give us the term "immortal bard"), and years before had galloped off to London, where Raleigh awaited death in the tower.

The mystery deepens for, as this goes on, Ben Jonson stages a mock funeral for Marlowe, convincing a minor poet to take his place for the burial. Ben Jonson is not to be confused with Samuel Johnson. He was Samuel Johnson. Samuel Johnson was not. Samuel Johnson was Samuel Pepys. Pepys was actually Raleigh, who had escaped from the tower to write *Paradise Lost* under the name of John Milton, a poet who because of blindness accidentally escaped to the tower and was hanged under the name of Jonathan Swift. This all becomes clearer when we realize that George Eliot was a woman.

Proceeding from this then, King Lear is not a play by Shakespeare but a satirical revue by Chaucer, originally titled "Nobody's Parfit," which contains in it a clue to the man who killed Marlowe, a man known around Elizabethan times (Elizabeth Barrett Browning) as Old Vic. Old Vic became more familiar to us later as Victor Hugo, who wrote *The Hunchback of Notre Dame*, which most students of literature feel is merely *Coriolanus* with a few obvious changes. (Say them both fast.)

We wonder then, was not Lewis Carroll caricaturing the whole situation when he wrote *Alice in Wonderland*? The March Hare was Shakespeare, the Mad Hatter, Marlowe, and the Dormouse, Bacon—or the Mad Hatter, Bacon, and the March Hare, Marlowe—or Carroll, Bacon, and the Dormouse, Marlowe—or Alice was Shakespeare—or Bacon—or Carroll was the Mad Hatter. A pity Carroll is not alive today to settle it. Or Bacon. Or Marlowe. Or Shakespeare. The point is, if you're going to move, notify your post office. Unless you don't give a hoot about posterity.

ACKNOWLEDGMENTS

Isaac Asimov for "The Immortal Bard." Copyright © 1957 by Isaac Asimov. First published in *Earth Is Room Enough* (1957). Reprinted by permission of the author.

McGraw-Hill Book Company for "Shakespeare's Life," from *Twisted Tales from Shakespeare* by Richard Armour, pp. 3–6.

The Society of Authors for *The Dark Lady of the Sonnets* by Bernard Shaw on behalf of the Bernard Shaw Estate.

Copyright © 1942 James Thurber. Copyright © 1970 Helen W. Thurber and Rosemary T. Sauers. From *My World— And Welcome To It*, published by Harcourt Brace Jovanovich.

A. P. Watt Ltd, for "Lady Macbeth's Trouble" by Maurice Baring, from *Unreliable History* on behalf of the Trustees of the Maurice Baring Will Trust.

Agents for the Estate of Caryl Brahms and S. J. Simon for "The Naming of the Globe," from *No Bed for Bacon*, by Caryl Brahms and S. J. Simon, p. 3.

Harcourt Brace Jovanovich for "Mr. *K*A*P*L*A*N* and Shakespeare," from *The Education of H*Y*M*A*N K*A*P*L*A*N* by Leonard Q. Ross.

Dodd, Mead & Company, Inc., for "Ring Out, Wild Bells" from *Bed of Neuroses* by Wolcott Gibbs.

Faber and Faber Publishers for "The Skinhead Hamlet" from *Not 1982* by Richard Curtis.

W. H. Freeman and Company for "Shakespeare the Physicist," by Banesh Hoffmann, Copyright © 1951 by Scientific American, Inc. All rights reserved.

Doubleday for "pete the parrot and shakespeare," from *archy and mehitabel* by Don Marquis.

Manson Myers for pp. 33–36 of *From Beowulf to Virginia Woolf.*

Random House, Inc., for pp. 201–15 from *Ulysses* by James Joyce.

Grove Press, Inc., for pp. 101–26 from *Rosencrantz and Guildenstern Are Dead* by Tom Stoppard.

Random House, Inc., for "But Soft . . . Real Soft" from *Without Feathers* by Woody Allen.